Wallace and Georgette Groves
We Thank You

Chapter One

The Ball

At the Golden Anniversary Ball celebrating the creation of the "Magic" city of Freeport, Grand Bahama, final tributes for its founder, the late Wallace Groves, were concluding.

Mr. Groves' eldest daughter, Gene, was speaking of what an incredible business man her father had been. She added that Wallace and Georgette Groves were wonderful parents to her and her siblings, Gayle, Graham, Gordon, and Gary. She also acknowledged several other important contributors to the success of Freeport, including Sir Jack Hayward. After Mr. Groves left Freeport, Sir Hayward and Edward St. George carried on the control of Freeport via the Grand Bahama Port Authority.

My twin sister, Brenda and I were at the Ball as Gene's guests. We have been friends of Gene since we were teenagers in Freeport.

I sat at a table near the front of the huge ballroom with Sir Hayward's son, Rick Hayward and his wife, Alex, as well as other members of the Groves' family. Brenda sat at the front table with Gene and other honored guests, including a descendant of Winston Churchill.

The British were a huge part of Freeport. In fact, Queen Elizabeth II had been invited to this fantastic event, but the Mistress of Ceremony announced that the Queen's RSVP had been received and the Queen would be unable to attend.

Dinner entrees included Dungeness Crab Soup with Sherry Cream, Caribbean broiled lobster and filet mignon with citrus butter and port wine sauce. Dessert was chocolate brandy mousse with a passion fruit cream.

I savored the sweet, delectable lobster. The abundant lobster found in the clear waters of the Bahamas.

The tender lobster brought back memories of our dad, A.R. Smith, and our brother, Gary, snorkeling for lobster.

Lobster was incredibly plentiful in early Freeport.

We had at least 70 lobster tails in the freezer and Daddy knew how to cook it. He would broil it and serve it with lemon and drawn butter.

After the accolades, I mingled with other guests at the edge of the dance floor. We chatted about how wonderful Freeport was in the early years.

I noticed two young men bound onto the dance floor to dance with young girls who had been part of the night's entertainment.

I was mesmerized by the young men as they danced with wild abandon. They were handsome with sandy brown hair and seemed oblivious to the admiring stares surrounding them.

Twins, I realized.

When they left the dance floor, I asked one his name.

"Rupert Hayward," he replied, in an upper-crust British accent. He also introduced his twin brother, Giles, and their beautiful sister, Francesca. I realized these gorgeous siblings were the children of Rick and Alex Hayward.

"I had not realized that Sir Hayward had *twin* grandsons." I said. "And… I hesitated, there was another set of twins in the early days of Freeport…"

Chapter Two

Runaway

Brenda, our brother, Gary, and I winced hearing our father, A.R. Smith grumble about the cost of gas as he drove us toward Silver Cove beach. Despite owning five houses in the Bahamas, and property in the U.S., Daddy was very frugal and loved to complain about prices of this or that.

As we headed the last two miles toward the beach, we were suddenly surprised to see a riderless horse, racing back towards the stable. A Bahamian trail guide rode in desperate pursuit trying to catch the runaway horse before it crossed dangerous Sunrise Highway.

I shouted, "Stop the car and let us out!"

Brenda and I jumped out of the barely-stopped car. Brenda managed to get to the horse and grab its reins. She patted it, and confidently mounted the excited horse as the guide caught up to them.

"Finders, keepers!" she joked to the relieved guide.

The guide said, "T'anks Ma'am, my name is Jameson. Brenda said, "Hi Jameson, I have seen you at the stable. My name is Brenda and this is my sister, Linda." I waved at him and got back into the car. Brenda and Jameson rode the horses back to Silver Cove.

Gary and I grinned at each other at the successful capture as Daddy drove to the beach.

At Silver Cove, we saw the rest of the group of riders - a father and two girls. The girls looked about nine or ten years old. One young girl was bent over brushing sand off of her jeans.

While she was doing that, the other horses, knowing one had run away, were prancing nervously. The riders were nervous too, and the horses sensed it.

One horse decided to join in the mischief. It suddenly did a mild buck and its rider fell off. She landed in the soft sand as her horse bolted in the direction of the stable. Fortunately, I was already out of the car, and, through sheer luck, caught the naughty horse

"Whew! That was close!"

"Girls, if you want to ride your horses back to the stable, my sister, Brenda and I will lead them all the way," I said.

However, the young girls were too unnerved at this point.

"Don't worry, if it's okay with your Dad, you can ride back to the stable in our car. Brenda and I will ride the horses."

Their Dad, said, "That's a great idea, Thanks!"

Once at the stable, the relieved guide said, "T'anks ma'am, you don't know how bad it be if dese horses run into the fas' traffic of de Sunrise Highway. Las' time, we have to call de 'meat wagon.' You pro'lly saved some lives today."

I blushed and said, "You are welcome! I like your horse, what is his name?"

He told me the big red gelding was named Lance. Jameson added, "He for sale."

A wonderful thought filled my head. I had just started a job as a Junior Computer Programmer at Island Data Processing.

My next step would be to realize my life-long dream; I would get a horse of my own!

Chapter Three

Insane with Joy

Saturday morning, I awoke to the sound of birds singing as if they were insane with joy. I shared their joy as I anticipated returning to the stable to check on Lance and any other horses that may also be for sale.

I showered and dressed in jeans, a T-shirt, and some short boots. As I stepped out of our guest house, I admired lush bowers of yellow trumpet flowers that spilled over the fence. I could also smell the sweet fragrance of jasmine and gardenia as I reached the main house.

Our home in Freeport is sleek and modern. It has a long, flat-roof and the house features two white limestone walls. One wall anchors one end of the house, and the second wall bisects the house at about three fourths the length of the house. This second limestone wall provides the interior wall of the den.

Both walls extend slightly from the house on the outside. One end of the den has narrow redwood doors and golden smoked glass.

We can open these doors for a nice breeze. The main house has three bedrooms and two baths.

There is also a two-bedroom, one-bath guest house, in the back, that sets at an angle to the main house. We used one bedroom for guests, and the other bedroom was used for Pam and me.

We had a large family, and it was great to have plenty of room.

Brenda opened the back door of the main house and greeted me. "Happy Saturday!" she exclaimed.

"Same to you," I replied.

As I entered the house, the warm, buttery-syrupy smell of pancakes greeted me. Our younger siblings, Pam and Gary were in the kitchen where Gary was flipping pancakes.

Fifteen-year-old Gary loved pancakes – besides it was the only thing he knew how to cook. He had made stacks of pancakes that Pam and Brenda were eating.

"Morning everyone! Ready to get a horse?!" I exclaimed as Gary poured more batter into the hot skillet.

Brenda quipped, "It's about time there was a real horse in this family!"

Brenda and I had been horse-crazy girls. As children, our record number of horse pictures on the walls was sixty-three. We both dreamed of owning a horse one day. Now, the dream of getting a real horse was within reach!

Pamela said, "I wish Carole could go with us today!"

We all missed our beautiful, older sister, Carole who had married a man named Bill Smith a couple of years before. Carole looked a lot like a young Sophia Loren. We would sometimes hear a rumor that Sophia Loren was on the Island, and we would laugh as we knew it was very likely Carole.

A famous Italian movie director saw her and told our mother that he would write a movie specifically for Carole.

Mom nixed the idea.

Therefore, instead of becoming a movie star, Carole married Bill Smith, a man twelve- years her senior, and they lived on the Island in one of Daddy's rental houses.

Today, they were visiting Bimini for a few days.

Mom and Daddy were also travelling today. They were already at the Freeport airport and would fly on the company plane to Tennessee. Mom would visit some of her family, and Daddy would purchase a fifty-acre farm.

Although we had several cars, our parents wouldn't let any of us drive if they were off the island. So, after enjoying the pancake breakfast, I called a taxi.

The stable is only about two miles away and it only took a few minutes for a friendly, Bahamian driver to drop us there.

None of us could contain our excitement, eager to see the horses.

Chapter Four

Pinetree Stables

We were all familiar with Pinetree stables. The stable was within walking distance of Freeport High School, and horseback riding was part of our Phys-Ed class. Our class would walk the short distance to the stable, and each student would ponder which horse to ride. Myra, the British woman who owned the stable, would always offer suggestions as to which horse was best for each rider.

Once the horses were assigned we would have a wonderful time riding the two miles or so to Silver Cove beach.

It was the greatest fun riding the horses into the pristine waters of Silver Cove!

Myra, knew we were coming to see the horses. When we arrived, she came out of the office. "Good morning, everyone," she said in her lovely British accent. I hear you want to see some of our horses that are for sale."

"Yes!" we all replied in unison.

I said, "I saw Lance, yesterday, but would like to see any other horses, too. I brought along Brenda, Pam, and Gary to help me choose."

"Lance is for sale," Myra said.

We saw Lance, already saddled and tied to the hitching post. "And I can show you two mares that are also for sale. Jameson, bring the two mares, please."

Jameson had already anticipated the request and lead two mares up to us.

One mare was a small brown mare named Russian Roulette. The other horse was a tall, grayish mare that was alarmingly thin. Myra said, "We haven't named her yet, but may call her Topaz."

We each took turns riding the horses.

Lance was a big red gelding. Muscular and dependable. He was a decent ride, too. Pam liked him. However, he was older than either mare, possibly a decade older according to Myra but he was an easy ride, doing everything we asked him to do.

Russian Roulette was in excellent condition and was also a very easy ride. She was very push-button.

Gary really liked how easy she was to handle and it was very tempting to make him happy by choosing a horse he liked.

The third horse looked bad. For some unknown reason, her coat had been shaved off, and her body looked grey. She had a thin white mane and tail.

I could see the vertebrae in the mare's back and the points of her hips were missing hair. She had a thin neck, and narrow chest. However, I knew enough about horses to see that she had excellent conformation.

Although she allowed me to ride her, I could tell her heart wasn't in it. I could also tell that she was gaited and was a very smooth ride. She was also the youngest of the three horses, at just four years old.

Brenda wanted her.

I was undecided.

"She is a palomino." Myra said. "Her dam is a gaited Cuban Walker."

"Let me show you her dam so you know what color she will become when her coat grows back."

I followed Myra to a nearby stall where a small, gold mare stood. She, too, was slightly underweight but I could see that she had excellent conformation and I loved her color. She was the color of a gold doubloon.

"She is gold, and her daughter will be gold, once her coat grows back." Myra added.

Despite the thin mare's condition, she cost one hundred dollars more than the other two horses.

It was time to decide.

Deciding was tough. Each horse had its own merits.

Gary liked Russian for her push-button control. She was a perfectly acceptable choice. Lance was also a good choice. I liked how bomb-proof he was.

Brenda said, "I really like the big, skinny mare, Linda."

Pam exclaimed, "I like them all!"

I had a momentous decision to make!

I finally chose Lance but could not buy him on the spot.

"Myra, I want Lance, but I need time to go to the bank on Monday to get the down payment for him."

"That will be fine," Myra replied.

That night, at home, I changed my mind. Despite the extra cost, I decided to buy the skinny mare, instead. She was the youngest of the three horses, and she would be palomino once her coat grew back. She was also gaited like her Cuban Walker mother.

Brenda clapped her hands in excitement when I told her.

That night, I could barely sleep. I wrote in my diary, *"I hope she is a good horse."*

Monday, I put money down, and signed a contract to pay for the young mare, an English saddle and bridle, and the monthly boarding fee. I had waited all of my life for this moment. Everything in me *knew* how right this bold step was.

I took a deep breath as joy and supreme happiness engulfed me.

Chapter Five

Mine

My new horse's stall was the first one in the long line of stalls at Pinetree stables.

As soon as I signed to buy the emaciated mare, I grabbed a brush and hurried to her stall. She barely paid attention to me as she ate her oats. I softly glided the brush over her bony hips and carefully brushed her prominent ribs.

I was already madly in love with *My* withdrawn and very hungry mare. *Mine, Mine!* The thought overwhelmed me with joy! My *Dream*, my *Happiness*, right there in the clean stall!

The mare eagerly ate, ignoring me.

That night at home, my twin sister, Brenda, who is also my best friend, and I talked excitedly about what to name my new mare. Golden Girl? Topaz? Del Oro...?

Then Tom Jones came on the radio singing the heart-wrenching love song, "DELILAH." "Why, Why, Why, Delilah? My, My, My, Delilah."

"That was it! I will name her Delilah!" I exclaimed, but, I want *gold* in her name." The name "Merrylegs" popped into my head.

Merrylegs was a small pony in the book, "Black Beauty."

Merrylegs, Merrylegs, no...Delilah Merry...gold! DELILAH MERRYGOLD!! I repeated it a couple of times...that was it!

Brenda said, "I LOVE it! Now let's fatten her up!

At the stable, I discovered why Delilah was in such bad condition. She and her mother had been rescued from a stable at Eight Mile Rock that had gone out of business. Delilah's coat was in such rough condition that Myra had it shaved off revealing the dark gray skin underneath.

I went into my depressed mare's stall and said, "I will take care of you, girl, ... don't worry!"

I kept my word and fussed over every aspect of Delilah's care. Although the barn employees kept the stalls very clean, I would often repeat the cleaning.

Then, I would carefully groom Delilah and give her apples as a snack.

Sometimes, I would even sneak a handful of grain from the closely-guarded feed room for her.

In time, with proper feeding and the extra supplements that Myra recommended, Delilah began to regain her health. Her grey coat started turning gold as it grew out.

Delilah's vertebrae no longer showed as she gained weight.

Within weeks of buying her, Delilah's short, thin neck seemed to lengthen and curve as she gained muscle tone. As she gained weight, she also started showing more energy and spirit.

I love a spirited horse, and the first time I rode Delilah to gorgeous Silver Cove, she bunny-hopped a little before settling down into a wonderfully smooth ride.

Her gait was thrilling and so comfortable.

As a gaited mare, Delilah would never do the jarring trot other horses do. And, she rarely broke into a run. She would just cover the ground with a beautiful, natural rhythm. A sort of pacing that was very fast.

She could easily speed past a running horse.

I was delighted with her.

She was part of the magic that seemed to be everywhere on the peaceful island.

Chapter Six

The Smiths

Our family consists of our parents, A. R. Smith and Gloria Smith, our older sister, Carole, my twin Brenda and me (Linda), and our younger siblings, Pamela and Gary.

Although Daddy was in the Navy, our parents made certain that we always lived off the Navy bases in large homes with a lot of room to run around. They wanted us to live off-base so that we could get to learn about other cultures and become friends with local children.

Mom made motherhood look easy. She had six children, four in diapers by the time she was 21 years old. She has a quick wit and tremendous energy and a very sharp mind.

And she is very beautiful.

Mom made our childhood fun. She always says that her headstone needs to read, "*We had Fun, didn't we?*"

We had lived most of our young lives outside of the U.S.A. mostly in tropical areas such as Hawaii and the Philippines, and we were used to being close to beaches. In fact, we lived at 808

Manila Boulevard in a huge house that was right on the beach in the Philippines.

Our parents used to travel to Hong Kong, where they would have clothes made for themselves.

Mom looked like she could be a movie star. To add to the look, she would cut out a picture of a certain dress some movie star was photographed in and take it to some of the incredible tailors in Hong Kong. They would replicate some of the finest dresses in dazzling fabrics. All tailor made to fit Mom.

She had one suit made, that we particularly loved. We call it the "Tomato Suit." It is the color of a rich, ripe tomato. It is fitted at the waist and the skirt comes down just below the knee.

One pink dress that Mom had made to wear to her 30th Birthday party was always called the "Pineapple Dress." It was made of some light, airy fabric, and a pineapple fiber was used to embroider flowers onto the skirt. Mom loved that dress!

Of course, she also had the classic silk Oriental dresses in black, red, white, and blue.

She also loved polka-dots as seen in this photo of her and

Daddy. They already had six children by the time this was taken.

The best part of growing up as a Smith is that our family was large. There was always someone to do things with.

Siblings are great but having Brenda as my twin has added the most fun and adventure to my life. We got a real love of travel from our parents and as we got older, we travelled every chance we got. We always had fun.

Mom's wit and sense of fun was passed on to all of us including our younger siblings, Pamela and Gary.

L to R Pamela, Linda, Carole and Brenda.

They both have delightful and comical senses of humor. Pam and Gary went to Mary Star of the Sea. Pam ran track, and as she got older, modelled bikinis.

Gary was a fun, mischievous baby brother. As time went on, he started dating, and eventually married Alison Drake, the love of his life.

Gary was "cool, calm, and collected." No matter how dire the situation, he could out cool Clint Eastwood.

He was also smart and kind.

When he was about five years old, we lived in a large house in the Philippines. The house was directly across the street from the ocean and was elevated on pilons.

The garage was under the house. So was the doghouse with our dog and her litter of puppies.

Sadly, one day, mom accidentally ran over a puppy that had escaped from its pen.

It was Brenda's black and white furry puppy, and she was inconsolable.

Without anyone asking him to do so, Gary brought his puppy to Brenda and handed it to her.

That was Gary.

Kind, sweet, and generous his entire life.

Pamela Smith above. Gary Smith and Alison Drake below.

Chapter Seven

Moving to Freeport

Brenda's notes:

Our father, A.R. Smith, took a position in Freeport, Grand Bahamas in Air Traffic Control with a company called The Grand Bahama Port Authority. The next thing we know, our family, and our dog, Melody, are on a Mackey propjet as it droned east out of Miami, towards Freeport, Grand Bahama where Daddy is waiting for us. Linda is sitting next to me, and our dog, Melody is on my lap.

Twenty-five minutes out of Miami a long strip of land appeared. It was so narrow, I could see the ocean on both sides. It was Grand Bahama Island. I later learned the island is about eighty miles long, and seven miles wide. As the plane approached the island, I could make out a small airport. Thin pine trees lined both sides of the runway. Just past the far side of the runway, the land turned into marshy ground and then into ocean.

The aircraft landed and taxied to the airport.

One by one we stepped off the plane into shimmering waves

of humid heat rising from the tarmac. We walked to a long, low pink building that had a sign "Welcome to Freeport."

Once inside the airport, we noticed two paintings. One was of Queen Elizabeth II and the other was Prince Philip. The island had been a British colony for three centuries.

Daddy was waiting for us once we cleared Customs.

He drove a car to the front of the Customs exit to pick us up. The car was a blue, faded-to-battleship-gray Datsun that was shaped like a German helmet and smelled of sunbaked leather.

Our entire family couldn't fit into the small car, and a fellow Air Traffic Controller, Ray Roberts, took the rest of us to our new home.

He had a British accent.

As we left the airport, we noticed that Ray drove on the left side of the road, the way they do in England and, instead of "STOP" signs, the signs read, "HALT AT MAJOR ROAD AHEAD." We never saw a major road and laughed every time we saw that sign.

We continued down narrow side roads and encountered quite a few potholes. Occasionally, we would hit a pothole, and greyish-white water would splash up from the street.

One sad note is that we saw several sick dogs along the roads. We also saw men putting a sick dog into the trunk of a car. We later learned there was a distemper outbreak.

The woods along the roads consisted of thin pine trees everywhere and some short Sago palms and palmettos in the underbrush. We had lived in the tropics and expected Grand Bahama to look like a tropical paradise. However, the island was sparse, bare, and uninviting.

Things became more disappointing when we pulled into the driveway of a small concrete-block house. The yard was gravel, limestone, and sharp stickers. No trees, no grass, no flowers-same as the neighboring houses.

We went into the small three-bedroom, one-bath house.

It was quite a contrast to our large brick home on seven lush acres in the U.S.

We had massive trees, including pine trees and some of the trees had purple wisteria winding all the way up them in the spring. There were also: peach trees, cherry trees, mulberry trees, pear trees, plum trees, and all sorts of delicious berries growing on the seven acres. The branches on the pear tree were so heavy with pears, they would break.

Daddy kept a few beef cattle, and we had a freezer full of home-grown beef. He also grew all sorts of vegetables, including tomatoes, turnips, and corn.

Glass jugs of milk were delivered every few days. Cream floated on top of the milk, and on winter days, the cardboard seals on the glass jugs would be pushed up by icy crystals in the milk.

We soon learned that the abundant, fresh foods that we were used to would just be a memory in the early Freeport days. The small grocery store had very limited choices.

One item that we could never adjust to was the milk. There was no fresh milk. Instead there was a box of white powder called "Reconstituted Milk." Just add water…

Chapter Eight

Wallace Groves and Early Freeport

There can be no mention of Freeport, without referring to its Founder, Wallace Groves. Groves was a brilliant businessman who had a logging company on Grand Bahama Island. His brilliance was validated by the fact that he earned five degrees from Georgetown University, which he obtained in two years.

When he was young, he was referred to as the "Boy Genius."

His yearbook from Georgetown University has a comment from one of his fellow classmates saying the best thing that happened to him and his classmates is that they got to be in classes with Wallace Groves.

Wallace Groves was very familiar with the Bahamas, as he not only owned the logging business on Grand Bahama, but he also owned the private island of Little Whale Cay, which he purchased in the 1930's.

Groves realized that the sparsely-populated Grand Bahama Island had incredible potential if it were developed. At only about

76 miles from Florida, it was perfectly located to become a thriving vacation spot.

The main tourist destination in the Bahamas was Nassau, the capitol of the Bahamas. However, Nassau, on New Providence Island, was a lot farther from the U.S. and New Providence was much smaller than Grand Bahama.

The Bahamas was a British Colony, so Wallace Groves met with representatives of Britain and the Government of the Bahamas to draft a plan for the development of Freeport.

The plan, called The Hawksbill Creek Act, was signed into action in 1955. It granted 50,000 acres of Crown land to be developed by Wallace Groves.

Groves brought in big investors such as D.K. Ludwig, Sir Charles Hayward, and Keith Gonsalves.

Mr. Groves and his family knew Charles Hayward.

The Groves were on their private island of Little Whale Cay when a large yacht moored nearby.

It was the Hayward yacht.

Mrs. Groves invited Hayward and his family to have lunch on Little Whale and a friendship/business relationship developed.

D.K. Ludwig was another huge addition to the plans to develop Freeport. He dredged the very important deep-water Harbour.

This Port would be able to accommodate huge cruise ships, as well as military ships from various governments. Most ships were British naval vessels.

The Port would be overseen by The Grand Bahama Port Authority.

Roads also had to be designed and built.

Doug Silvera was instrumental in helping to build the well-laid-out streets of Freeport.

Groves also brought in an influx of construction companies as there was a desperate need for more housing.

Other than company concrete-block houses there were almost no houses on Grand Bahama other than a few in the small Bahamian villages.

Even Wallace Groves and his family had to stay in a hotel, The Caravel Club, while their mansion on the beach was being built.

Groves hired the gifted architect, Alfred Browning Parker to build his home.

The Hayward mansion, was also built during this time, right next to the Groves home.

Freeport, had to be built from the limestone ground up.

GROVES TURNS ON FIRST TRAFFIC LIGHT
...another sign of growing city

Chapter Nine

We Fall in Love with Freeport

After the initial shock of moving to a place most people had never heard of, we started to make friends in the neighborhood.

The Sheerans were one family that was very similar to ours.

Norma and Ed Sheeran had a blended family of four daughters and one son and we Smith kids were always having fun with the Sheeran/Hall kids.

Brenda and I became good friends with their eldest daughter, Donna Hall, while Pam and Gary hung out with the younger siblings.

Norma and Ed Sheeran were wonderful parents to them, and Ed Sheeran, eventually became head of the Freeport Telephone Company.

There was also a family of boys just up the block from us – the Rose boys. They were athletic, and good looking and knew every inch of the Island.

We were all beginning to settle into Island life.

One of the first hopeful signs that we would be able to adapt to living in Freeport came on the day Mom and Daddy drove us to the beach.

Daddy drove down a road that had more skinny pine trees on either side. As the car rounded a slight curve we were stunned by the unbelievable beauty of the beach!

Transparent aqua water and deep blue water sparkled in the sun like all the world's wealth spread out before us. We may as well have been prospectors that had come upon a vast lake of aquamarines and sapphires sparkling in the desert.

We ran across the white sand to the water's edge.

The water was as clear as cellophane and we could see our toes as clearly as if we were standing in a bathtub at home. We splashed deeper into the warm water until we were about chest-deep and could still see our toes!

We started doing something we had not done much of since our arrival – smiling. Our teeth looked whiter as the sun tanned us.

The second sign we had that we could settle here was the discovery that there was a horse stable on the Island!

Brenda and I loved horses and used our babysitting money to rent them to ride on the same gorgeous beach we had just been to.

Things only got better, when our wonderful Freeport High School was built, and horseback riding was part of the curriculum!

Another surprise was that even the scarcity of items in the grocery store turned out to have a silver lining.

Because of the shortage of items in the stores, we developed a genuine appreciation when we did find whatever rare item we were searching for.

For example, if you managed to find the last box of chocolate-covered cherries at Christmas, or the last box of chocolate marshmallow eggs or even egg dye for Easter, it was a *huge* deal!

Or you would search aisle after empty aisle, and suddenly spy the last box of Valentines candy setting alone on a shelf. You would rush to it, looking around, furtively, hoping no one else was making a bee line to it.

When you went home, you hid the treasure and complained about not finding anything – only to surprise the recipient later.

If we had been in the U.S we would have taken it for granted that we could always find whatever Holiday goodies we wanted.

Chapter Ten

British School

Brenda, Carole, and I were enrolled in a small British School called St. Paul's where we were taught by a truly international group of teachers. Most came from England, like our Physics teacher Mr. McNeill and Headmaster, Mr. Lord. Our History teacher, roly-poly Mr. Jagodinski was from Poland, I think, and had a tall, slender French wife.

The Headmaster, Mr. Lord, was a hard-edged, old-school Brit. He was very strict.

The Nuns at Mary Star of the Sea Catholic School were also very strict. They taught our younger siblings, Pamela and Gary as well as most of the younger students in Freeport.

Students at our school were also an international mix, mainly European as well as Chinese students and Bahamian students. There was a set of Chinese twins, Penny and Cheryl Cheatow.

Brenda and I, being twins, bonded immediately with Penny and Cheryl.

All four of us had long dark hair and Mr. Lord noticed.

When the students and faculty gathered in the auditorium to sing, "God Save The Queen", Mr. Lord made it clear that anyone with long hair had to make certain it was put up before going into the Science Lab.

"Immediately!"

Spoken by Mr. Lord, the word came out *'Em Med Jet Lee.'*

Well, the Cheatow twins complied, but Brenda and I didn't always follow the rules. Brenda and I got a warning at first, then we got sent home.

I forgot one too many times and was sent to the office to be disciplined by the Headmaster, Mr. Lord.

That meant *The Cane.*

I was very scared and nervous knowing I would have to meet with Mr. Lord, but, to my relief, he was not in the office.

In his place, stood our physics teacher, Mr. McNeill, cane in hand. He said, "Hold your hand out, please."

I did so, palm up, expecting the painful slash of the cane at any moment.

Mr. McNeill never raised the cane. He simply said, "You may return to class."

Chapter Eleven

Headmaster Mr. Davies

Brenda's notes:

We had a new Headmaster at the newly-built Freeport High School named Hugh M. Davies. Mr. Davies was a very short, balding man who wore a Headmaster's black cape. As he walked briskly up and down the hallways, his black cape would swirl out behind him, in a Dracula-like fashion. If you caught a quick glimpse of him flying by, you could swear you saw a huge bat. A bat with a crisp English accent and strict British rules.

I saw an example of how Mr. Davies ruled when I volunteered to work in the school office.

The Freeport High School secretary was a young British woman named Mrs. Cumine. Mrs. Cumine was tall, willowy, and wore mini-skirts which were the hip *MOD* British style of the day. Her hair was short and red. She was married to Mr. Cumine, the math teacher.

Her husband, too, was also hip and very attractive. He was always well-dressed and was tall, dark and handsome, and drove a white Chevy convertible with a black top.

Occasionally Mrs. Cumine would leave early on Friday and, if needed, a student could volunteer to cover for her.

One Friday I volunteered for this duty. It was a nice change of pace and allowed me to get out of class for a while.

On that particular Friday, I sat at Mrs. Cumine's desk, doing some light organizing of paperwork that I would file. Her desk was just outside of Headmaster Davie's office.

A young male student was sitting awaiting a meeting with Mr. Davies. He had been sent to the office for slapping a girl in the face.

The young man was tall and muscular, and probably a half-foot taller than Mr. Davies.

The phone on the desk rang. It was Mr. Davies. "Send the young man in, please."

I ushered the student into Mr. Davies office and closed the door.

I could easily hear the conversation on the other side of the door (the wine glass pressed to the wall helped).

I could hear the student tell Mr. Davies, "I didn't slap her that hard."

Mr. Davies responded in his formal British accent, "Did you slap her this hard? Followed by the unmistakable sound of a *SLAP*. "Or did you slap her This hard?" Followed by an even louder *SLAP*!

My blood froze as I expected a violent reaction by the student. The student, however, said nothing.

At this point, Headmaster Davies simply talked to the young man, in a kind tone, telling him it is *never* OK to hit a woman for any reason.

He sent the student out of the office, but not before shaking hands with him.

I admired the Headmaster for his courage, and kindness.

He wanted the young man to know what a slap felt like and he also wanted him to learn, early on, that that kind of behavior wouldn't be tolerated, in school or in the world at large.

We students were taught to respect our teachers and other adults. We had to stand if either one entered the classroom. This respect clearly carried over to this student because he didn't *DARE* fight the Headmaster.

Mr. Davies also helped the female students with a problem in the Girl's Room. The janitor had reported that the Girl's Room was always a mess with things strewn around, lipstick on the mirrors, toilet paper on the floor and sometimes even unflushed toilets.

Mr. Davies called all of the girls into the auditorium. He brought up the subject of the disorder in the Girl's Room. I expected him to berate us and call us names.

Instead, he told us that we were important, that we were the *next* generation. Our children would look up to us and follow the examples that we set. We needed to show respect for others such as the janitor, and for the property itself.

After Mr. Davies treated us like adults, the Girl's Room was never left in disarray again.

I learned why Headmaster Davies wore a cape. He was not a bat, but a Super Hero!

Chapter Twelve

Boomtown

As time passed, Freeport, Grand Bahama Island was becoming an exciting and dynamic boomtown!

The largest Holiday Inn in the world was built. The Lucayan Beach Hotel and Casino were completed. Every inch of Freeport was eventually landscaped and immaculately maintained. Many beautiful homes were built, and we moved into a gorgeous, very modern home that had plenty of room for all of us.

Freeport was also very safe. Crime was something we rarely heard about unless we listened to the news from the U.S.A.

As a young girl I would walk home late at night after babysitting. The only light was from the moon.

The Island also had the Rand Memorial Hospital, and many good Doctors, including the Antoni brothers.

The Antoni Doctors were three handsome brothers who were renown on the island for providing excellent medical and dental care to anyone who needed help.

I have heard that in the early days of Freeport, they might let a patient stay on their couch or one of the Antoni Doctors would make a house-call to the patient's home.

They later built the modern smoked-glass, glamorous Antoni Clinic on Sunrise Highway.

Another highlight of the boom was the opening of the Humane Society of Grand Bahama and a Veterinary office in Freeport.

Now people could get their pets vaccinated and protected from the horrors of distemper.

Freeport was quickly becoming the Riviera of the Caribbean.

Thousands of British, Bahamians and expatriates were thriving as new companies and jobs flooded in.

There was also the Freeport Players Guild for people in the community who had been bitten by the acting bug.

The Guild was a vibrant place, originally located in a Quonset hut, and featured surprisingly talented members of the Freeport community, including Dr. Amado Antoni's son, Kirk Antoni.

Kirk looked as "handsome as Elvis Presley" when he was on stage. (Or off stage!)

The biggest patron of the Guild was Sir Charles Hayward's son, Jack Hayward, who sponsored the new state of the art building for the Guild that had the mechanics to lift actors into the air or make them disappear into the stage floor.

By 1967 the International Bazaar had been built on at least ten acres. It was a splendid complex of shops, restaurants, and businesses.

The shops had first-class stores such as: Baccarat, Gucci, Cartier's, Emeralds of Columbia, and incredible clothing boutiques.

It felt as if you were in different countries as you strolled through the streets of the International Bazaar. There was the Madrid Café where you could watch Spanish Dancers and eat Paella. Or you could find yourself in Scandinavia or Istanbul.

Mom and our older sister, Carole, loved to shop in the French area.

Carole would carefully choose French lingerie and Mom would buy French perfume. Mom's mother spoke French, so it seemed a natural place for her to shop.

There was also a wonderful coin shop where we all bought coins over time.

One of the main attractions of the International Bazaar was the Japanese Steak House and the large green Hoi-Toi. The imposing statue is similar to a Buddha. It was a tradition on the island to get a photograph of yourself standing next to the 'Buddha.'

Japanese Steakhouse.   Donna Hall and 'Budda'

Some of the finest hotels were also completed and bustling with thousands of guests.

The King's Inn was a dramatically beautiful hotel near Randfurly Circus (a circular round-about in the road several miles from the airport.)

Its lawn featured a waterfall, bridges, and tall coconut trees. The trees were lighted with lights in greens, reds, and blues.

The King's Inn also featured a pool that had a modern white sculpture that towered above it. The giant sculpture could be seen from quite a distance and the pool often had movie stars lounging around it.

The King's Inn and its large manicured lawn were directly across from the International Bazaar and El Casino.

El Casino was a luxurious place that also had movie stars and very sophisticated men and women dressed in their finest tuxedoes and evening gowns.

Most of the croupiers in the casino were handsome Italian men. These men were as fit as polo players and added a lot of sex appeal wherever they went.

Being in the El Casino was like being in a James Bond movie.

Freeport became a microcosm of the World. People from all over the world either visited or lived there.

Everyone lived in harmony and there was an exciting pioneering spirit throughout the Island.

It was a place where Wallace Groves said, "One can be happy, before it's too late."

Chapter Thirteen

Bahamians

One of the best parts of being in the Bahamas is the Bahamian people. They are friendly and light-hearted with a sense of happiness that is contagious.

Their island accents are lilting and lovely and there is a refreshing common sense in much of their conversations.

Once when Mom and I were at the Airport in Miami, heading back to Freeport, the flight was delayed for mechanical repairs.

Several Bahamians were also heading back home.

We were getting a little nervous about the safety of the flight.

One smiling Bahamian woman turned to us and said, "Don't worry about de plane, the first to go will be de Captain, so he will make sure de flight is safe."

Bahamians have strong family bonds, and their children are usually very delightful and polite.

Men and women usually dressed in sophisticated fashion, more European than Island. They are more likely to wear leather shoes, rather than athletic shoes, and the women are more likely to wear real gold earrings rather than costume.

Many of the Bahamian women worked in the banks and offices of Freeport. Others worked in the fabulous perfume shops and busy airline counters. Some worked in private homes, restaurants, and hotels.

One Bahamian woman was hired by A.R. Smith and was sent to the U.S for training to become an Air Traffic Controller.

When she returned, she worked for years in the Freeport Tower.

The Taxi business was busier every year and many men made their living driving taxis. They were kept very busy by the approximately 200,000 visitors to the Island each year.

Booming Freeport provided hundreds of jobs for unskilled labor, also.

Hundreds of men (I read 500) were employed in keeping the newly-minted city absolutely pristine. Its landscaped areas were vast, starting at Freeport International Airport and going all the way to the Lucayan Beach.

I used to say that you could give a blind person a camera and let them take photos in Freeport, and it would not be possible for anything but beautiful photos to be taken.

There would be "street" dances downtown, and one of the popular songs at the time was "Downtown."

Music of the sixties was unsurpassed with the Beatles predominating, but the island music was the most fun.

One of my favorite songs, other than "Island in The Sun," is "Limbo Rock." We saw a lot of limbo in Freeport, and also enjoyed the rousing tradition of Junkanoo every year.

Bahamian friends introduced us to hearty peas and rice, conch fritters, and conch salad.

Conch is said to have a tranquilizing ingredient in it.

I think the sound of steel drums is also soothing.

No wonder we all walked around relaxed and smiling.

No matter how big the problem, we all adopted the "No big t'ing mon." philosophy.

Chapter Fourteen

Currency in the Bahamas

British Sterling was the formal currency used in the Bahamas. However, U.S. dollars were always welcome as well.

As a result, we not only had to do transactions in U.S. dollars, but also British Sterling.

Math homework consisted of lots of adding, subtracting, and multiplying in fourteens. At the time, a shilling was 14 cents. A ten-shilling note was $1.40, and the pound note was $2.80 cents.

There were other interesting coins such as the thruppence (three cents) pronounced *tuppence*, and the half-penny (pronounced *ha'penny*) was worth half a penny. The smallest coin was called a farthing. It was worth ¼ of a penny, was stopped being used in 1960.

If a person were referred to as a "farthing" it was not a compliment.

By the mid 1960's, the Bahamas developed its own currency-currency that rivaled the beauty of the Islands.

The dollar bill was a soft green, with a picture of Queen Elizabeth II on the front of it, and an underwater scene on the back.

There was a delightful, red three-dollar bill with the Queen on the front, and a beach scene on the opposite side.

The coins were unusual, also.

The 1966 silver dollar had Queen Elizabeth II on its face and a conch shell on its reverse side.

There was a diamond-shaped 15 cent piece with a hibiscus on it, and also a charming dime with scalloped edges. The dime had Queen Elizabeth on one side, and two sharks on the opposite side.

All three currencies were accepted in the Bahamas.

Chapter Fifteen

Conga Line

Brenda's notes:

The first job I had while still in high school was working at the airport for a company called Intercontinental Realty. The company had a booth in the main lobby of the airport facing the entry doors. I sat behind the desk and people would come over and I would take their address if they wanted more information on buying real estate in the Bahamas.

It was a very easy and fun job, and the fact that Linda worked at Penny-Farthing sundry shop, mom worked in the perfume shop (until she was hired by Eastern Airlines) and daddy was in the Air Traffic Control tower made the airport feel like a home away from home.

The airport had a restaurant at one end that served delicious club sandwiches. There were also souvenir shops and a perfume shop.

Friendly Bahamians with beautiful voices and smiles staffed the airline counters and the Customs department as well as the very busy taxi stand.

I loved to people watch at the airport.

One lady came into the lobby in a see- through dress made of macramé. She had every luggage handler fighting to carry her luggage.

Movie stars and other celebrities would pass through the airport almost daily. Dionne Warwick, Robert Taylor, Bette Davis, (her daughter lived on the island) Sidney Poitier, and Bill Blass.

Sidney Poitier asked me to go to dinner with him, but I was too shy to say yes. Bill Blass, who was a new designer at the time, asked me to come to the Lucayan Beach hotel to model some of his dresses. Again, I turned him down for the same reason.

Music was always on the overhead speakers. Songs by the Beatles and the theme from James Bond could be heard.

One day the song "Tequila" played over the loudspeakers. The beat of that song is absolutely perfect for . . . a conga line!

Someone spontaneously formed a conga line which snaked throughout the airport, growing in length as people left their posts to join in. Such was the spirit of the island.

Takeelah!

Chapter Sixteen

Hurricanes

The Bahamas were often threatened by hurricanes, as the storms formed off of Africa and made their way Northwest towards the U.S.

Whether Bahamian, or expatriates, we all became one as we faced storms that threatened us all.

I remember helping several Bahamians tape windows at the Freeport International Airport. There was a strong sense of comradery as everyone helped each other do what small preparations we could as the storm neared.

The storm, in this case was named Betsy.

When the Airport closed, there was a sharp feeling of fear, mixed with courage as the last escape route off the Island was gone. We all knew that we were in this together and could only depend on each other for survival.

Although the airport was closed, our dad, A.R. Smith, would stay alone in the control tower in case any aircraft were lost in the coming storm and needed help.

At first, Betsy skirted most of the Bahamas, and seemed headed to the east coast of the U.S.A.

However, she took a turn south back towards the Bahamas!

We were still living in the concrete-block company house in 1965 and would ride the storm out there.

However, we still had to pick up our sister, Carole who was working in the gift shop at the Lucayan Beach hotel.

Mom and I drove through heavy rain and winds to get to the hotel to bring Carole home. We were shocked to see ocean water rushing across the road closest to the hotel.

We drove through it.

Carole was waiting for us in the elegant Lucayan Hotel lobby.

She had bought a bag of some of our favorite candies, including Cadbury chocolates -Dairy Milk, Fruit and Nut, and Whole Nut. She had also bought Crunchie, and our favorite coconut and chocolate candy called Bounty!

We hurried home before the ocean swamped the road completely.

We could hear the winds howling, and rain was lashing everything in its path.

As the storm intensified, the rain started blowing through the concrete walls on one end of the house! We removed wall hangings and huddled in the living room. Water would come in near the top of the wall and run down to the floor. It was a relief when the storm abated a few hours later.

At least in Freeport.

Betsy was very damaging to Nassau. A tourist ship named the Yarmouth Castle had just docked in Nassau.

Wisely, its Captain moved the ship out to sea away from the storm and managed to successfully ride out the storm.

Betsy turned *again* and entered the Gulf of Mexico. She had traveled over 2,000 miles in 10 days.

Grand Isle, Louisiana, was wiped out by Betsy, and over 400 boats were grounded or sunk by the storm. Betsy was the most expensive storm up to 1965.

The name, Betsy, had been used previously, during an earlier hurricane season.

After the Betsy of 1965, the name was retired.

Chapter Seventeen

Brenda

My twin sister, Brenda would make a great heroine in a novel. Her looks alone, would qualify her, but her class, wit, and sense of adventure only add to her charm.

She looked like a young Bridgette Bardot, if Bardot had dark brown hair and green eyes and a joyful smile on her face.

Brenda was born with a love of learning. She had Reader's Digest in French, Spanish, and English. She would eagerly study the language differences in the books.

Brenda also had a wonderful sense of style. Even as a child, she was very careful about her clothing and belongings.

As a teenager, she would carefully shop some of the wonderful clothing boutiques in Freeport. She didn't have a lot of clothes, as we wore uniforms at Freeport High School, but everything she owned was stylish and carefully cared for.

Her favorite dress store was Evelyn's of Lucaya.

I remember one time, she put her hair up and carefully secured pheasant feathers in it.

Most people could never carry off such a dramatic touch, but she made it look absolutely *right.*

Brenda designed a gold ring for herself. It had a square top, with a heart carved in it, and her initials in script inside the heart.

Each of the four edges of the square had five hearts adding to twenty with the large heart on top being the 21st heart. She had it made for her twentieth birthday.

She wrote several companies in the U.S trying to find one that would create her ring. Credit cards didn't exist, and who would trust a stranger across the ocean to make payments?

Miller's of Colorado did.

Brenda mailed her drawing of the ring, and Miller's did an artistic job of translating the drawing into the 14-karat gold ring.

Brenda is also very artistic.

At Freeport High School, there are three places in the school office, for student's artwork. Usually two of these places held oil paintings or sculptures by Brenda.

It was a joy to watch her in a Museum such as the Louvre. She would become completely entranced in an artist's work and would remember everything about it even years later.

As for being a heroine, she was absolutely fearless about horses, or travel, or, well – conquering the world!

One day Brenda, went to Pinetree Stables and asked Myra for "the wildest horse you have." Myra was hesitant at first. However, she had seen Brenda ride a couple of the difficult horses at the stable.

One, a half-wild pinto, had run away with its terrified rider and jumped a small sports car on its way back to the stable. The horse's unpredictability was fine with Brenda. Her motto was, "Just don't give me a dull horse!"

Myra decided to show Brenda a horse that the tourists were not allowed to ride. She took Brenda to a stall at the back of the stable. Brenda was disappointed when she spied what looked like an old gray nag in the stall, but gained hope when Myra told her the old gelding's name *Crazy Grey...*

Crazy Grey seemed calm, but once Brenda saddled him, she said, "He becomes a fire-breathing dragon." Brenda would wrap the reins around her gloved hands and Crazy Grey would charge toward their destination. Brenda didn't force him forward or ride him hard, in fact she spent most of the ride holding him back.

Even so, froth came from his mouth and speckled his chest during their regular rides to the beach. Crazy Grey grew to look forward to these beach rides with his dauntless rider.

Brenda on Crazy Gray FPO, Bahamas

Brenda was intrepid in ways, yet very shy in others. Once when we babysat together, the father harmlessly said, "You are beautiful young girls." Brenda almost fled getting behind me as if to hide.

She barely looked around me, as I said, "Thank you!

Chapter Eighteen

Christmas in Freeport

Although there was no snow, Christmas in Freeport was as magical and special as any snowy scene from a Dickens' novel.

Commercial Christmas trees were not available in early Freeport, and it was intriguing to see the creative ways people came up with for their trees.

For a few years, we used an aluminum tree that we shone a multicolored light on.

One Christmas, Brenda and I stopped at a fellow high-school student's apartment where she lived with her family. The apartment was tiny, and yet the family had made room for a small Christmas tree that set on a table in the corner of their kitchen.

What was particularly delightful, is that instead of Christmas decorations on the tree, someone had painstakingly placed long balloons in between each soft branch of the tree. How the balloons had not popped is beyond me.

Another friend had a tall piece of driftwood which gracefully branched upwards, from a limestone planter. The driftwood looked great with Christmas ornaments and twinkling lights wound around the bare branches.

Midnight Mass was also a very special time. Our family, especially Mom, would dress up for Mass. Our Mother is always glamorous, and particularly at Christmas.

One Christmas, she wore a red suede dress which she

accentuated by wearing her set of emeralds from Emeralds of Columbia.

Father Brendan would conduct Midnight Mass at church on Sunrise highway.

At one point, we would all go outside and gather under the twinkling star over the Nativity. Father Brendan concluded the Mass at that moment, and we all got wonderful kiss on the cheek from the Antoni Doctors. As teenagers, we really looked forward to this tradition. Afterwards, we all went home and continued our tradition of having a glass of champagne or wine and opening one gift. We were so happy.

One of Brenda's favorite toasts was, "I would rather live in a shack in the Bahamas than a mansion anywhere else."

Brenda and Mom our house in Freeport.

Penthouse

Linda at home Bahamas

Chapter Nineteen

Linda

Brenda's notes:

I am so embarrassed by Linda's compliments about me, that I told her (threatened her) that I insist on adding my view of her.

She talks about my beauty, yet we are Twins! If I was so beautiful, so was she!

I know she isn't trying for any "reflection" onto herself, yet she seems to think I am the most fabulous person on the planet.

She is a fabulous person in her own right.

She seemed oblivious to compliments she would be given, in all sorts of ways. Not just for beauty, but for real brains. As years passed, she has solved major problems for Banks, and for several offices she worked in for FedEx in different states, including a problem that was nation-wide and costing the company a fortune!

One time she was walking down the beach wearing a green one-piece bathing suit. Two men walked past her, and one said, "Class, Pure Class."

She jokes that he said, "Ass, Pure Ass."

Chapter Twenty

Miles Berkeley

Brenda's notes:

We were acquainted with the British sailors early on in our Freeport years. That is because each Christmas, the residents of the island were encouraged to host a dinner for a few of the young sailors, as they were so far from home.

We would ride with daddy in our red and white Ford station wagon to the harbor where a British ship with an "HMS" title for "Her Majesty's Ship" lay alongside the dock. Usually we would invite three sailors home for dinner. The sailors were so young, usually eighteen or nineteen, thin, and polite.

They were always on their best behavior.

One young sailor, Miles Berkeley, stood out. Miles was incredibly articulate and brilliant. At only 20 years of age, he was writing a book on British Naval tradition.

Miles was from the Berkeley family in England. Berkeley, Virginia, Berkeley University, and Berkeley Castle are named for his family line.

Miles developed at serious crush on my sister, Linda. He had exquisite penmanship and wrote the most romantic letters to her.

Example of Miles Berkeley penmanship.

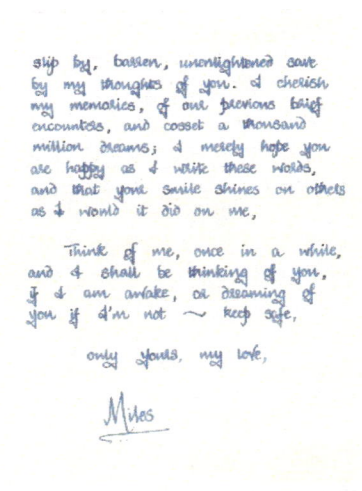

> slip by, barren, unenlightened save by my thoughts of you. I cherish my memories, of our previous brief encounters, and cosset a thousand million dreams; I merely hope you are happy as I write these words, and that your smile shines on others as it would it did on me,
>
> Think of me, once in a while, and I shall be thinking of you. If I am awake, or dreaming of you if I'm not ~ keep safe,
>
> only yours, my love,
>
> Miles

Some letters would be at least thirty pages long, and so beautiful that Linda considers them Art.

She treasures every one of them.

Chapter Twenty-one

The Pub on the Mall

Brenda's notes:

The Pub on the Mall is another incredibly popular place near the International Bazaar. It is huge and "Veddy" British.

As its name states, it is a Pub. Pub is short for 'Public House' or as we would say in America, bar.

The Pub is not your average bar. It is a large, two-story Tudor-style building. There is a huge front room with a fireplace at one end where rough slabs of beef were cooked over an open flame. The fireplace has a large coat-of-arms, hanging high up on it. Some of the walls of the Pub are covered in English scenes, and medieval items such as chastity belts and mace.

Mace is not a can of spray. It is a heavy round piece of iron on a chain and has spikes that can split a knight's armor open.

There were also three-feet tall glasses on display, which are used for serving a "yard" of ale. As the name suggests, the glasses are, indeed, a yard in height. That's a lot of ale! I've seen young

British sailors turn up a yard of ale and struggle to swig it down, as they slowly sank to their knees in their bell-bottomed uniforms.

There is a heavy, carved wood bar which is hard to see as it usually has people five and six deep bellying up to it. On nearby walls are dart boards, the traditional pub game. There was always a game or two being played by cheerful people vying for the winning spot.

There is also a balcony with tables where one can overlook the people and activities below.

British accents are the majority, but there are wonderful accents from many corners of the world. Laughter rings out everywhere.

At the back of the Pub, there is another large event room.

When our sister Carole eventually married, her wedding reception was held in this section of the Pub.

Her wedding was a big deal in the early days of Freeport. Flowers and other wedding items were not available and had to be flown in from Florida.

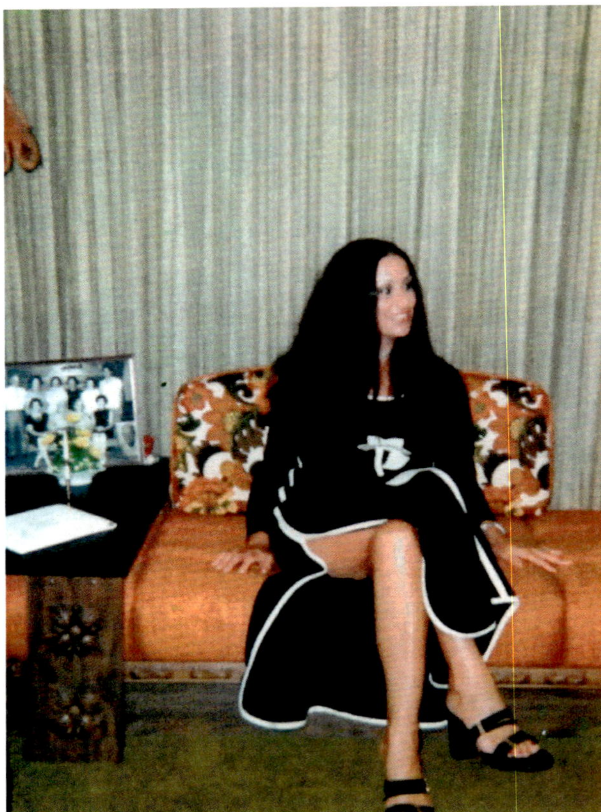

Chapter Twenty-two

Carole

Our older sister, Carole was our hero when we were growing up. She was protective of us and taught us a lot about becoming young ladies. Brenda and I would watch her carefully dab the smallest amount of a perfume called Tabu onto her slender white neck. Or we would watch her remove big curlers from her thick black hair.

When we moved to Freeport, Carole eventually started very informal dating, usually with groups of friends, or, if she went out with a young man, Brenda and I would usually go with her.

On one occasion some of her friends invited her to a large party at the Lucayan Beach Hotel. Carole was only in her teens, and didn't have any real evening wear, so she bought a fabulous bolt of blue silk satin. The material was the color of the light blue Bahamian water.

Carole hand-sewed a floor-length evening gown for the affair. She looked like Sophia Loren/Snow White as she stepped out with her friends. She had a rich red lipstick on her generous mouth and her dark hair was a perfect contrast to her gown.

As the evening proceeded, Carole saw Dr. Robert Antoni at the party. They spoke casually. She realized, by the end of the evening, that she and Dr. Robert were the only sober people in the room.

Chapter Twenty-three

Alcohol

There was no drinking age in Freeport. As teenagers, we could go into any nightclub and order drinks. We didn't have a problem at all sticking to one drink, usually a sweet, fruity Island drink like Planter's Punch.

I had learned at 14, that I didn't like to overdo alcohol.

It started the evening Brenda and I went with Carole to a young man's apartment to watch T.V.

The apartment must have been the scene of a party the night before. There were bottles of whiskey, glasses, full ash trays and half-finished sandwiches.

I was at that stage of early teen-hood where I could be dramatic.

I had never had alcohol, and no one noticed when I filled a large glass with some kind of dark whiskey. I downed it. Since I was still sober 30 seconds later, I poured another one, and downed it.

That is all I remember until the next day.

Brenda had noticed my foolishness and she and Carole put me in the shower trying to sober me up. The evening dragged on as everyone tried to right the situation. They took me to the soccer field and walked me for miles trying to sober me up.

Finally, Carole knew that we all better go home.

The thought was terrifying, as our parents are very strict.

When Carole and Brenda brought me through the door, Mom was waiting (like a cat switching its tail).

Carole lied, and said that her date had a small drink in the car, and I had drunk it. Mom raised her eyebrow as high as it would reach, and in an incredulous tone said, "One drink???!"

Mom's eyebrow has never come down since.

Brenda never let me live it down, either. Until she learned her lesson at an Island wedding.

Somehow, she thought of champagne as some kind of harmless carbonated beverage.

She was with our younger sister, Pamela, our brother Gary and one of his friends. They all went to the beach after the wedding, and only realized that Brenda had too much champagne, when she decided she would try to swim to Miami.

Gary and his friend pulled her out of the water by her arms and dragged her to the car, as her feet left long furrows in the sand.

The next morning, Brenda awoke on the floor of our guest house bathroom and it took a while before she could open more than one eye.

Fortunately, we both learned early how *not* to drink.

We had no problem at all being very moderate from then on.

Chapter Twenty-four

Robert Kennedy Shot!

Brenda and I were about to turn 18 on June 4, 1968, which was not only our Birthday, but also a British Holiday, called WHIT Monday. It was very rainy because a small hurricane named Abby was meandering near the Island.

We didn't have school that Monday, so we picked up some sweet and sour pork and fried rice from Jack Wong's and spent a lot of time watching T.V. Some of the Sheeran girls came over to have cake and ice cream with us and after they left, we kept watching TV.

There was a lot of news about Robert Kennedy and his political run in California. Robert Kennedy is ahead in the California primary.

We hope he wins!

We went to bed, only to awake to the news that Robert Kennedy was *Shot*! Kennedy had just won the California Primary, when someone on the kitchen staff shot him with a 22- caliber pistol! He had a serious wound to his head, and a superficial wound to his shoulder. He was in surgery 3 hours and 40 minutes and was still in a coma as of 12 noon. He is in very critical condition.

"Mom, if he dies, may Brenda and I go to the funeral?" "Yes, she replied. But we hope he will make it."

Five people were also wounded by gunfire as pandemonium broke out in the Embassy room of the Ambassador Hotel in California. The would-be assassin was almost killed by the crowd, but the Police quickly ushered him into a car.

The next morning, June 6, 1968, I awoke to hear that Robert F. Kennedy had not survived. He died at 1:44 am Los Angeles time and will lie in state at St Patrick's Cathedral on Friday.

Brenda and I made arrangements to go to Washington D.C. for the graveside service. We flew from Freeport to Miami on the 3:30 pm Eastern Airlines. From Miami, we took a direct flight to New York.

In New York, there were only small feeder aircraft to Washington, D.C. There was a long, long line of people trying to get to D.C. Brenda and I were at the back of the line and unlikely to be able to board the plane before it filled up.

Brenda

Suddenly an airline representative appeared in front of us, and said, "Follow me." He took us to the head of the line, and we boarded a very unusual airplane. At the front of the plane, there was an elevated area of seats that faced the rear of the plane. About two-thirds of the rest of the cabin had seats that faced forward. We were seated there.

I sat next to a preacher, and a teenager. An exhausted-looking man was talking about being at the Ambassador Hotel when Kennedy was shot. He looked tired and disheveled.

A man named Allen Peck was sitting next to Brenda and offered us a ride to our hotel once the plane landed.

We were straight out of our safe island and thought nothing of accepting the ride! Mr. Peck drove us around Washington in his white Mercedes before dropping us at the Marriot Hotel.

On June 7, 1968, the day before the funeral, Brenda and I decided to go visit Arlington Cemetery.

I dressed in a white skirt and a pink-striped blouse. Brenda dressed in a blue pantsuit which made her look like a Vargas girl.

We took a taxi to the Capitol and strolled around taking photos. We took photos in front of the White House and took the elevator to the top of the Washington Monument.

There was an impromptu campground of tents and plywood shelters nearby that was called Resurrection City. It was a demonstration against poverty. It was one of the last protests Martin Luther King had planned before he lost his life in Memphis. Robert Abernathy now headed the protest.

We continued to the Lincoln Memorial, and, since we had not had breakfast at the hotel, we found a nearby restaurant where we ate some waffles.

There was a flower woman outside of the restaurant and we bought eight red roses and white carnations.

Brenda and I then took a taxi to Arlington National Cemetery. We easily found the Eternal Flame of John F. Kennedy's grave and left the carnations on it.

The next day, we attended the grave-side service for Robert F. Kennedy. We were among hundreds of people there.

We all were entranced by Andy Williams singing a heartfelt rendition of "Ave Maria."

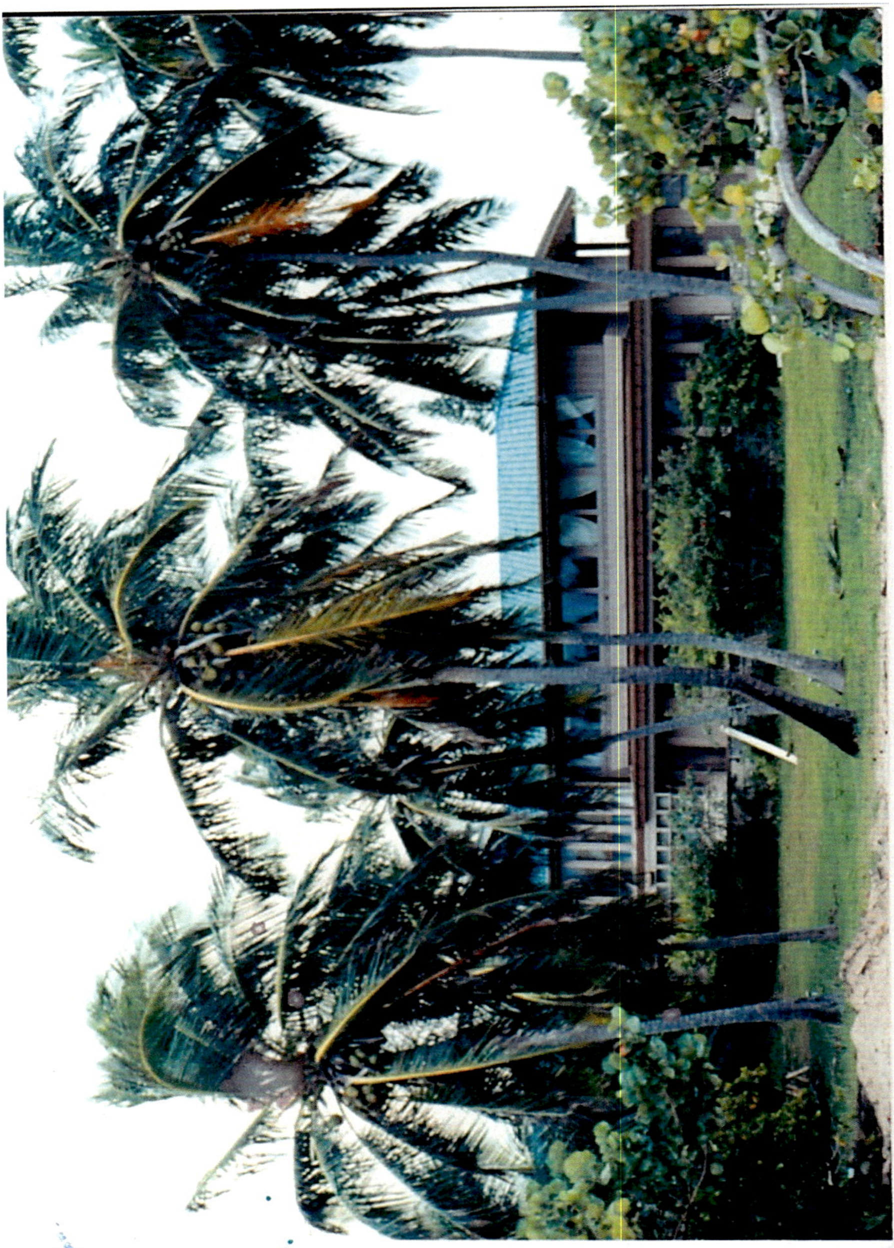

Chapter Twenty-Five

Blue Angels

Although both Brenda and I spent a lot of time with Delilah, we still made time to spend with friends. Gene Groves is one of our best friends. She is the eldest daughter of Freeport's Founder, Wallace Groves and his wife, Georgette.

Gene's siblings were off the Island in various schools around the world, and Gene was being tutored at the Groves' beach-front mansion rather than attending Freeport High School.

Georgette Groves decided that Gene was isolated in the huge home.

Gene's tutor, Mr. Jagodinski, was also our History teacher at Freeport High School. Mrs. Groves asked him if he could recommend any Freeport High School girls that had good reputations and were close in age to Gene.

Mr. "Jago" knew that Gene loved horses and so did we. He recommended that Gene meet us!

Soon afterwards, Brenda and I were called to the FHS office, where we were introduced to Mrs. Groves.

"Hello girls," she said. "Hello Mrs. Groves." we replied in unison.

We couldn't have been more surprised if Queen Elizabeth II had sought us out at our High School.

She further surprised us by inviting us to a small cocktail party the Groves were having for the Blue Angels. She added, "You can also meet our daughter, Gene. She is about the same age as you."

Like most young ladies, we were enthralled by the Blue Angels, and gladly accepted her invitation.

An invitation to the Groves' home was akin to a smaller version of an invitation to Buckingham Palace.

Mrs. Groves asked us how we liked Freeport High School and said she was considering putting Gene into the school.

We replied, "We love Freeport High School!"

After exchanging phone numbers, Brenda and I headed to the school parking lot. Classes had ended, and a few fellow students were admiring the green Chrysler Imperial with the license plate "14" on it. Mrs. Groves' car.

Brenda and I were uncertain at first if we would like Gene, or not. We knew we couldn't be '*friends*' just because of how incredibly important the Groves' family was so we were a little nervous.

Gene was probably nervous to meet us, too.

It was early afternoon as Brenda and I drove to the Groves' oceanfront mansion to meet Gene and the Blue Angels.

We were very excited as we drove up to the gate and used the intercom to announce our arrival. When we drove through the gates and parked, we saw Gene waiting for us on the wide white granite steps at the front of the home.

She smiled and said, "I'm Gene, thanks for coming! "Gene, I'm Brenda, and this is Linda.

"Hi Gene" I said, grinning. It's great to meet you! We love the Blue Angels!"

"Me too!" Gene replied.

Gene was very beautiful. In fact, she looked a lot like the actress, Candace Bergen. She was tall with honey blond hair, and really deep sapphire-blue eyes fringed with black eyelashes.

We hit it off immediately.

The three of us walked up a few broad steps and entered a large arboretum. The floor of the arboretum is white limestone. There are trees and tropical plants in the middle of this area. There is also a sparkling swimming pool on the left. As we continued past the arboretum, we entered the home itself. The floor is white marble. Directly in front of us was a cozy seating area in front of a white limestone fireplace. We all joined the handsome Blue Angels in this area.

As teenage girls, we were giddy. The Blue Angel pilots were handsome and immaculately groomed from their shiny hair to their polished shoes.

They knew we were young and flirted innocently.

Mr. Groves told them that our Father, A.R. Smith, was the Director of Air Traffic Control at the airport. They realized they had already met him when they first landed at Freeport International Airport.

Gene took some photographs of us as canapes and beverages were served. The canapes were salmon and cream cheese in a flaky triangle pastry and chicken Kiev bites.

Once in a while, I would momentarily unglue my eyes from the famous pilots. I glanced at the rug, and noticed it had the initials WG at one edge of it.

When one of the handsome pilots asked what we liked to do on the Island, Brenda said, "Ride horses!"

L to R: Captain Fred Craig, Lieutenant Norm Gandia, Brenda Smith, Lieutenant Frank Mezzadri.

Photo by Gene Groves.

Chapter Twenty-six

Gene

Brenda and I have had many wonderful adventures with our friend, Gene Groves. We met when we were only about 16 years old.

One of my first memories of going somewhere with Gene was when her parents let her take me and Brenda to the great Captain's Charthouse Restaurant near Sunrise Highway.

In the 1960's a steak dinner cost about $6.

Gene, Brenda, and I were making our way up the steep stairs to the Restaurant and paused for a moment on the landing.

As a young teenager, I uncouthly asked, "Gene, Gene, how much money did your Dad give you to take us to dinner?"

She had probably heard that tiresome question often in her life.

She looked and me, and replied, "A quarter of a hundred."

The Charthouse was only one of the many places we went with Gene.

One time, when Gene had to fly to Miami for her yearly physical, Mrs. Groves sent us with her. I think she wanted to keep Gene safe.

Brenda and I had so much fun. While Gene went for long medical tests, we watched T.V. in our Four Ambassadors Hotel room, had lunch at the hotel, and spent time at the pool.

So much for Gene's safety. Instead of taking a cab back to the hotel, she was offered a ride by a man in a corvette convertible.

She took it.

When she arrived back at the hotel and told us, both Brenda and I said Georgette would kill us if she knew!

I don't think she ever found out.

Left page: Gene and Brenda at Four Ambassadors.

Above, Gene and me on return flight to Freeport, Grand Bahama.

This was not the only flight concerning Gene and me.

The Groves were flying to their private island of Little Whale Cay, to celebrate New Year's Eve and Gene invited me to go.

Brenda was not on the island at the time, and I had just promised a couple that I would babysit their children while they went out for a huge New Year's celebration in Freeport.

I was torn, but kept my word to the couple.

The Groves flew to their island and their pilot departed.

Just minutes after he took off for the return trip to Freeport, he had to ditch the plane in the ocean.

It had run out of gas!

Sometimes I consider what could have happened had I been on the aircraft.

The extra weight might have been enough to cause the plane to run out of gas just as it was about to *land* at Little Whale. There could have been a terrible outcome if that happened.

At least that is how I console myself that I didn't go.

Chapter Twenty-seven

Picnic

One weekend, Brenda, Pam, Gary and I decided we would have a picnic on the beach. Pam packed some apples, and turkey sandwiches, while Brenda cut up some celery and carrots for us to snack on. Gary put everything into a knapsack, including a large thermos of cool water for us and our dog, Melody.

Melody was a cross between a dachshund and some unknown breed. She looked exactly like a Rottweiler, including the short tail, only she was about the size of a dachshund. Fortunately, she had good proportions and her back was not too long, and her legs were not too short.

The five of us piled into a taxi and headed to the stable where I saddled Delilah while Brenda gave her a carrot. The beach was not very far, so most of us would walk to the beach while one of us rode Delilah.

"Gary, I will ride Delilah just long enough to cross Sunrise Highway. Then you can ride her the rest of the way to the beach, since you have to carry the knapsack." Brenda, Pam, Melody and I walked alongside Gary and Delilah. Melody loved to go to the beach with us, even if she had to keep up with a horse.

Once, I tried to put Melody on Delilah with me, but she definitely didn't want to ride! Then, I remembered an incident that occurred several years before when she was just a puppy. We were just kids and took her onto the roof of our house. Somehow, she fell from the highest point of the roof into a flower bed, below. There were bricks around the flowerbed, and, fortunately, she missed hitting those, and landed in some deep mulch.

As we neared the beach, we could smell the ocean air in the breeze. Soon we were dazzled by the beauty of the exquisite beach. It is always a thrilling moment to see what "mood" the beach was in.

Today, the water was calm and changed color from clear where is flirts with the beach, to a lovely relaxing turquoise where we do most of our swimming, to a deep- darker blue a hundred yards out. The water was gently lapping the shore, as a couple of people swam a short distance offshore.

We found a nice flat area in the soft sand.

I took Delilah's reins as Gary dismounted. He carried the knapsack to our picnic spot where Pam and Brenda had spread a large blanket on the sand. They started unpacking the goodies, while Melody started chasing a small crab as it scurried into its hole in the sand.

I gave Delilah another piece of carrot then climbed into the saddle for a ride along the water's edge.

Delilah pranced excitedly and bunny-hopped a couple of times before settling down to a smooth gait. I marveled at the comfort of her gait as we continued to the end of Silver Cove where we turned back and returned to the group.

Brenda said, "I want to ride next!"

"Okay, I said, as I dismounted. Be careful, she is very nervous and full of herself."

Not that I needed to warn Brenda. She was a great rider, and the person I trusted the most with Delilah.

I joined Pam and Gary near the food, and bit into a turkey sandwich.

"This is good, Pam!"

"Thanks," she replied, smiling.

Gary popped the last bite of his sandwich into his mouth and ran grinning into the inviting water of Silver Cove.

Pamela rode Delilah next. Instead of turning left down the empty beach, she turned Delilah to the right towards a couple of Bahamian shacks.

Delilah seemed very nervous.

"Slow down, Pam, let me check on her." I shouted.

I was still getting Delilah used to new experiences and took her reins. I lead her near the small houses, with Pam still on her.

A couple of young Bahamian boys excitedly pointed at Delilah. I stopped her to let them pet her.

They patted her and asked if she needed any water. "Thanks, I said, that would be great."

They filled a bucket of water from a hose in front of the small house for her to drink. Delilah touched the water with her muzzle but didn't drink.

However, she seemed to enjoy all of the attention from the delighted boys.

After we all took turns riding, I removed Delilah's saddle and led her to the smooth surf.

I laughed as Delilah pawed at the water, splashing it high around both of us. She buckled her front legs, then her back legs as she lay down in the shallow surf. She playfully rolled in the water, relishing the pleasure of this new adventure. Twice.

When she got up, she began shivering slightly. We had more beach towels, and we all rubbed her dry. She was still underweight, and I was careful not to over work her.

However, she was gaining weight and becoming absolutely beautiful.

BEFORE, Skinny, miserable-AFTER happy, healthy Delilah

Chapter Twenty-eight

Ugly Duckling

Everyone, including me, was surprised to see what a stunning mare Delilah was becoming. She quickly gained the nickname, "Ugly Duckling."

Several people tried to buy her from me, but my response was always the same.

"She will never be for sale."

I saw Delilah almost daily, but she paid no real attention to me at first. To her, I was just another tourist riding her and her heart was guarded.

As for me, I was in complete awe of her. I could not believe I owned such a magical creature. A mystical being. An- other-worldly unicorn.

I was even in awe of her inner workings; Her heart, her lungs, even her stomach growling. Her size and strength.

I even loved her big, round hooves.

Chapter Twenty-nine

The Eclipse and Rainbow

Everyone is so excited, because there is to be an eclipse of the sun today!

For safety's sake, all of the horses at the stable were put into their stalls, and even the top gates of the stalls were closed.

Tom, one of my brother's friends, offered to lend me his camera to view the eclipse. I told him that I would be at the stable, and probably not look at it. The radio warned people *not* to view it, even with filters. However, I was curious, and did try to view it through a hole cut into a piece of paper. That didn't work.

I stayed in Delilah's dim stall and groomed her during the eclipse.

Afterwards, I took Delilah for a short ride to Silver Cove.

Suzie Wells, a beautiful lady I used to babysit for, waved and I rode Delilah over to her. Suzie had never seen Delilah and stood looking up at me as I sat on Delilah.

Suzie exclaimed, "You are so *lucky*, you are so *lucky!*"

I felt lucky indeed as Delilah curved her graceful neck and pawed the sand next to Suzie.

"Thank you, Suzie!"

As Delilah and I rode away we seemed to float down the beach as a gorgeous, full rainbow appeared above the aqua lagoon.

The Magic of Freeport….

Chapter Thirty

Treasure Island

Freeport was a real Treasure Island, not only in its incredible beauty, but literally!

Divers found a sunken treasure just off of Lucayan Beach, in water so shallow that you could stand with you head out of water at low tide. They had discovered a canon with silver pieces of eight stuck to it.

Eventually, thousands of these silver coins from a sunken Spanish galleon were recovered within shouting distance of shore.

One of the divers wrote a book about the find, called "Finders, Losers." I think it can be found on Amazon.

In the early 1970's, I was able to acquire a piece of eight from the wreck.

I took it to a jeweler and explained that I wanted it made into a necklace for Mom as our parents were about to celebrate their 25th Wedding Anniversary-the Silver Anniversary.

I said, "I want the silver to represent 25 years of marriage, and I would like gold used to represent the future 50th year of marriage.

The jeweler wrapped the round edges of the coin in taffy-thick gold and was able to create a bezel to hold the coin on a long silver chain.

I told the jeweler that I would like something for Daddy, also.

When I told him that Daddy worked in Air Traffic Control, he showed me a small gold airplane and a thin, rough bar of silver.

He said, "I will bend the silver bar to create a tie bar. After I polish the silver, I will attach the gold plane to it."

"Wonderful! Please engrave the tie bar with, *Happy 25th Anniversary, Love, Linda.*"

Chapter Thirty-one

Sunday Dinner with Gene

One Sunday, when Mr. and Mrs. Groves were not home, Gene invited Brenda and me to come over for dinner. She asked, "Be here by 3:00, if possible."

When we arrived, Gene pointed out a small envelope that Mrs. Groves had left on the entry table for Brenda.

Brenda and Mrs. Groves had made a bet of fifty cents on the outcome of a car race. Brenda's choice had won, so Mrs. Groves had enclosed Brenda's winnings. There was a hand-written note from Georgette, *"I couldn't find fifty cents anywhere. I hope you can use this. Fondly, GCG."*

Enclosed, Brenda found a beautiful Bahamian Silver dollar key chain.

"I have a cold," Gene said, so I won't be swimming, but we can still walk on the beach. Let's have a snack, before we do anything!" She took us into their bar.

When we entered the bar, we saw a bar and bar stools to our left. To the right is a seating area consisting of sofas softly lit by table-side lamps.

To our delight, Gene had three plates of thick chocolate cake slices ready for us at the bar. We sat down and savoured the rich, chocolate cake. "Mmm." Gene laughed when I said, "Wow, you really know how to spoil us, Gene!"

After the delicious snack, we went walking on the beach.

Brenda and I walked on either side of Gene. A man suddenly appeared from the sand dunes to our left, and took several photographs of us, as we walked.

When we returned to the Groves' home, we were greeted by the smell of cookies baking. We headed to the dining room where there were appetizers of salmon, olives, carrots and celery served with hot bread and butter. The main course was filet mignon served with spinach soufflé, french fries, and corn.

What a feast Gene treated us to! We were thrilled by the wonderful dinner and it only got better, when dessert was served.

We had fresh raspberries in port, vanilla and chocolate ice cream, *and* warm cookies.

Chapter Thirty-two

Lightning

One day, I went to the stable to ride Delilah. She was in the pasture, and I whistled to her. She heard me and pranced gracefully towards me at the pasture fence.

She reminded me of a tall ship in full sail gliding across a calm sea. I am thrilled that she is beginning to respond to me.

I gently haltered her and led her to the saddling area.

"Hey D, ready to go to the beach?" I said as I lifted the English saddle onto her smooth back.

I replaced her halter with her bridle, then stepped up into the stirrup and settled onto the saddle. We turned toward the stable's gravel driveway in the direction of the beach.

After a couple of minutes, Delilah started to favor her right front hoof. As soon as I noticed the slight change in her walk, I stopped her and dismounted. I walked around my golden girl and ran my hand down her right leg.

Delilah knew that was the signal for her to lift her hoof and complied. I could see that a small piece of gravel had wedged itself between the hard hoof wall, and the softer middle part of her hoof. I gently pried it out of her hoof and she put her hoof down. I patted her and remounted. I was relieved to see that Delilah began walking normally and shuddered to think that a tourist riding her might not have noticed the subtle limp and would have continued the ride perhaps damaging Delilah's hoof.

Delilah breathed a deep sigh knowing the discomfort was gone and I felt her trust in me deepen.

We slowed as we approached Sunrise highway to make sure there was no traffic. I stopped Delilah, and we both turned our heads left and right to make sure we could cross safely. It was darling to see her head move in unison with mine. We carefully crossed the road and continued towards the beach.

Anticipation grew as we reached the narrow path through the sea grape bushes to the beach. This was always the place, the doorway where one always wondered what the beach would look like that day, that hour. It is *always* an exciting moment.

I smiled when I saw Delilah raise her head high and prick her ears forward in anticipation. I knew she was as eager to see the beach as I was.

Would the aqua water be placid and clear softly lapping the pristine beach, or would there be turbulent water stirring up seaweed and strewing it on the sand?

The wind grew stronger.

The wind was a warning, and a dark, stormy beach suddenly came into view.

Delilah tucked her rump under her and descended the slight incline through the sea grape path to the beach. We both inhaled the salt air as the wind whipped through our hair.

Delilah's white mane danced in the wind!

I could see heavy, dark storm clouds hanging off the shore. The biggest one looked like a huge, gray jellyfish in the sky with stinging tentacles that streamed down to touch the angry sea.

Somehow, one cloud was pink, and the very air itself seemed to blush pink. I could even see a slight pink reflection nestled in Delilah's white mane.

My heart beat faster as I felt an exhilarating surge of speed as Delilah paced down the deserted beach.

Suddenly, a crack of thunder and a bolt of lightning forced me to call off the beach ride. Heavy raindrops blowing sideways began pelting us as I turned Delilah back towards the stable.

Delilah easily leapt up the sand incline and burst through the sea grape portal as we fled the storm.

The storm seemed to be clutching at us threatening to drag us back, perhaps to sweep us out to sea, only to toss us lifeless on the beach when the tide gave us up.

Lightning struck so close to us that Delilah startled a second, but quickly gathered herself as she ran. We both knew, in a primal way, that we were in escape mode.

As Delilah raced back to the stable, I leaned forward and entangled my hand in her wet mane, all the while holding tightly to the reins. Heavy rain drenched us as I slowed her to make sure we could safely cross Sunrise highway. We crossed the highway and were back at the stable in minutes.

The weather had run everyone off, and the stable was deserted.

I knew I could not put Delilah into her stall, without cooling her down from the long run.

After unsaddling her, I led her up and down the covered hallways of the barn for about twenty minutes for her to cool down.

As if miffed that the storm had not engulfed us, lightning struck some nearby wires and caused a small arc of electricity to shoot from a nearby electrical outlet.

Right next to Delilah's face. A bit of a raspberry from the storm.

Delilah responded with a triumphant snort.

Whew, time to go home, I thought.

I put Delilah into her clean stall and rubbed her dry with a large beach towel. Fresh hay and grain were already in her stall.

She ate, contentedly, and for the first time, one ear was cocked back towards me.

"I see your ear. So, you finally know I exist?"

Chapter Thirty-three

Sandy Man

We loved horses and so did Gene. In fact, she owned the second horse to the Island, a small red horse named Sandy Man.

The Freeport News published the momentous moment when Sandy was delivered by barge to Freeport and met the first horse on the Island, Danny Boy.

A girl about Gene's age owned Danny Boy, and in the early days, she and Gene rode their two horses on the beaches of Freeport.

There was no stable at the time, and Sandy Man was kept on the three-acre property that was part of the Groves' ocean-front estate.

The Groves' home was designed for entertaining guests from all over the world, such as Prince Rainier and Princess Grace of Monaco. The home was stocked with everything needed to do so.

Some of the extra beverages, including wine and champagne, for these parties was stored in one of their garages.

When a hurricane was approaching, Georgette decided to put Sandy Man into the huge garage to protect him.

As the hurricane neared, Sandy Man panicked at the screaming winds and terrifying noises of the storm. He managed to kick the boxes of champagne, wine, and other beverages into a pile of pummeled boxes that were leaking various liquid refreshments.

Georgette was protective of Sandy Man, until Gene walked home from the beach, where she had been riding him. Gene had blood running down her face and there was a hoofprint on her forehead at the hairline.

Sandy Man was donated to the new stable on the island, called Pinetree, where he became a much-loved ride for many children.

Georgette Groves was also very protective of her children.

Georgette lived during the time of the Lindberg kidnapping and kidnapping may have concerned her. Some public photos taken of the Groves' children when they were young, show the children with their faces turned away from the photographers.

Georgette even saved 14 stitches in some rolled-up gauze from the appendectomy Gene had as a child.

Chapter Thirty-four

Yachting

Brenda and I always looked forward to calls from Gene. She usually had some fun time planned which included "the girls" as her mother, Georgette, referred to us.

One Saturday morning, Gene called and invited us to go out on the Groves' yacht, *The Gamma*.

The Groves loved the letter G in their names, and Gamma is Greek for the letter G.

She said, "We can fish, and then we'll have lunch on the boat. Dad has some friends whose sons will be there too! They are from Yale University. We will head out at 11 am."

"Sounds like fun, Gene!" I said." Brenda and I will meet you at the Marina. "

We had seen the yacht before when Gene had asked us to come see the "boat" her parents had bought. We had gone to the Marina, and there was a 60-foot yacht with the name "Gamma" on the end of it.

After we boarded the yacht, Dave Stolze, the yacht's Captain, carefully maneuvered the Gamma out of the harbor.

The water was breathtaking.

Besides being shallow, the Bahamian water is also known as "gin-clear." The water is so clear, we could see the patterns and colors of the coral reefs, and fish. The water sparkled in the sun, and it was easy to see through it all the way to the ocean bottom.

As we moved into deeper water, the water color changed from the lightest blue-green to a deeper blue.

Captain Dave set me up in one of the fishing chairs. "Keep this seatbelt on." he warned, as he fastened the seatbelt around me. He then showed me how to hold the professional fishing rig.

I needed his help. The only fish I had ever caught was from our boat a year earlier. It was a dazzling-colored angelfish. Once I landed it, taking it out of its element, I was shocked to see it turn gray. I rushed to put it back into the ocean.

The fishing rig suddenly felt as if the hook were bolted to the bottom of the ocean. I had caught something! But what? I pulled and sweated and laughed and struggled. I simply did not believe there was anything on the line other than a large coral rock. I was certain the line was somehow caught on something. However, Captain Dave insisted that I did have a fish on the line.

I had struggled at least 45 minutes, when Gene stuck her head up to the deck where I was strapped in the chair.

"Haven't you reeled it in yet?" she drolly chided. Lunch is

LINDA GROVES YACHT "GAMMA"
BAHAMAS
80 lb tuna

ready!" she laughed, as she took a photo of me struggling with the fish/rock.

Captain Dave put the yacht in reverse, and, finally, I saw that there was indeed a fish! A huge fish!

"She's caught a tuna!" one of the men exclaimed at they pulled it onto the boat. After the grand workout, I (the young woman and the sea) had with the fish, I undid my seatbelt and joined the others downstairs for a well-earned lunch.

In the dining area of the yacht, we all enjoyed roast beef with crusty bread, potato salad, and a plate of fresh-sliced fruit. We also ate walnut brownies Gene had made. We chatted with the Yale boys as we ate. One of the young men said, "I'm going to catch the next fish!"

True to his claim the young man reeled in a huge fish! It only took him about ten minutes.

Unfortunately, it was a large shark!

The men tried to release it back into the sea, but it didn't survive their attempts to remove the hook. I think someone mentioned it would be donated for bait at the dock.

Meanwhile, I took photos. Brenda always had innate-style. Today she was wearing the latest style in yacht wear – harem pants and a bathing suit top with a small vest over it.

The material was the lightest-weight, soft pink fabric. It was designed to let the wearer get a tan right through the fabric.

After this wonderful day in the incredible waters of the Bahamas, Captain Dave turned the yacht back towards the Marina.

Mrs. Groves had a professional photographer waiting to take a photograph of me and Brenda with the fish!

Then, some men on the dock filleted the tuna. They used sharp knives to make short work of my 80-lb tuna as they bagged the fillets in large, clear plastic bags for us to take home.

Many pounds of fresh, delicious fish!

We thanked Mrs. Groves and Gene and bid farewell to the college boys. Gene and her Mom headed home in the Groves' green Chrysler Imperial.

Daddy was thrilled with the tuna. He prepared some of the large square fillets with a light breading and deep-fried them.

He put the remaining fish into the freezer which already contained dozens of *rock* lobster he and our brother, Gary, had caught just offshore.

Chapter Thirty-five

Captain Dave

Sadly, the Captain of the Groves' yacht, David Stolze wouldn't survive the rest of 1970.

Later in the year, Captain Dave and some friends had gone out on the Gamma to enjoy a few hours of scuba diving.

Dave went into the water, and, despite being very experienced about the dangers of diving, he developed the painful condition called the Bends.

The condition is caused when the water pressure on the body causes nitrogen to dissolve in the blood. If a person ascends too quickly, the nitrogen expands in the body including joints, and causes severe pain. If there is no decompression chamber available, the only hope is for the victim to go deeper into the dive, and slowly, slowly ascend giving time for the condition to reverse itself.

There was no decompression chamber in Freeport, so Dave was rushed to the airport where a Coast Guard plane was waiting to fly him to Key West for treatment.

Sadly, Dave didn't survive the emergency and died. He left behind a wife named Linda.

He was only 27 years old.

The tragedy was very upsetting to everyone involved including the Groves.

As a result, Mr. Groves had a decompression chamber brought into Freeport to help prevent such a tragedy in the future.

Chapter Thirty-six

The Young German

Late one afternoon, when I returned to the stable from a beach ride on Delilah, I saw a handsome young blond man standing next to a bay horse. The sun was setting, and the stable was deserted except for the two of us.

He seemed on the verge of tears as he stood holding the reins.

"May I help you?" I asked.

He seemed distressed and replied in a thick German accent, "Ya, I cannot take this off of the horse," as he pointed to the bridle. "There is no one to ask for help."

I said, "I will be more than happy to help you, my name is Linda."

"Thank you, my name is C."

I showed C how to undo the buckle on the throatlatch of the bridle and explained that it is important to put one's hand at the horse's mouth to gently support the bit so it doesn't hit the horse's teeth.

I carefully lifted the bridle by the top strap just behind the horse's ears and pulled the bridle over its ears as I cradled the bit.

C was relieved and thanked me profusely. I admired the handsome, helpless young man.

After helping C, I turned to Delilah to take care of her before putting her into her stall. I led her around to the wash rack at the back of the barn and turned the hose on. As I rinsed the sand and salt off of Delilah, I reveled in her beauty. She now had a sleek golden coat, and a snowy white mane and tail.

After rubbing her dry, I led her back to her stall where she was eager to eat the grain and hay she knew would be there for her.

I sat down for a few minutes in the fresh pine shavings just to watch her eat. Her neck had a graceful curve now, and her snowy tail cascaded like a silver waterfall to the ground.

Delilah was the dream I always had since childhood and now my dream had come true. Only the reality was far more wonderful than I could have imagined.

I was filled with a sense of happiness, joy, and contentment.

Chapter Thirty-seven

Lady Willpower

Brenda's notes:

There was another golden mare at the stable named Lady Willpower. She was owned by a German family, and ridden by their daughter, Marion M.

Lady was very well-trained and athletic. She was often used in Polo games, or endurance competitions.

One day, Mrs. M wanted to accompany me on a beach ride.

I rode Delilah, and Mrs. M rode Lady Willpower.

As we rode at a slow pace, she confided that their family was going to have to leave Freeport. She added "In Germany we had to say, 'Heil Hitler', now we say, 'Heil Pindling.'"

"I'm sorry to see you go!" What a surprise! Will you be taking Lady with you? If she is for sale, I would love to buy her."

Mrs. M replied, "We have already sold her to our friends in Germany. They come to Freeport six weeks every year. I noticed what wonderful care you and your sister take with Delilah. Lady loves being ridden. I hate to think of her standing in her stall and missing the beach."

"I would love for you to consider Lady as your horse, except for the six weeks when we or her new owners come here on vacation. Treat her as if she is yours, but you won't have to pay her bills."

This generous offer resulted in both Linda and me having golden mares to ride and love!

Lady and I bonded quickly. She would kick her stall when she heard my voice at the stable as she was eager to be ridden to the beach.

One day I rode Lady to the far end of Silver Cove beach then turned her towards our target - a long stretch of hard sand edged by the crystal-clear water. The stretch of beach was framed within the space between her ears, almost like a rifle sight. I could feel her energy growing in anticipation of being free to run as fast and far as she desired. I took a tight grasp on her white mane. Looking down, I could see that my gold ring and her gold neck were the exact same color.

With an almost imperceptible cue from me, more mental than physical, Lady leapt forward. I was riding her bareback and no matter how hard I held on, I slid to her mid-back. In one stride, I pulled myself forward to where I started.

BRENDA & LADY BAHAMAS

Sand flew out from behind Lady's hindquarters as she dug in to propel herself forward. It flew high in the air like the waves behind a speed boat.

I felt pure joy.

We soared down the beach, barely touching the ground.

Brenda @ Lady, FPO, Bahamas

She practically outran her shadow as I let her run to her heart's delight.

After the run, I rode Lady into the water. She would walk in the shallow water, until it was deep enough to pick her up like a huge floating barrel and, with powerful strokes of her legs, she started swimming.

After the swim, I saw two young Bahamian boys on the beach. They wanted to swim with Lady.

We all went back into the water, and the gleeful boys hung onto the end of Lady's long tail, as she slowly pulled them through the aqua water.

Linda Smith on Delilah Merrygold left. Brenda Smith on Lady Willpower.

Our dog Melody under awning. Photo by Gene Groves.

Chapter Thirty-eight

Gene makes a hamburger

One day when Mr. and Mrs. Groves were deep-sea fishing on the Gamma, Gene invited Brenda, me, and our younger siblings, Pam and Gary, to her house for lunch. She said we could all swim and she would cook hamburgers for us.

There was an outdoor kitchen near the pool and Gene had all the items needed to make the hamburgers.

The rest of us slipped into the large, sparkling swimming pool. At least the girls did. Gary did a cannonball into the pool!

While we swam, Gene started preparing the hamburgers.

Occasionally, I would get out of the pool, and watch Gene cook the hamburgers. She had shaped them into perfectly round, baseball-sized balls. She put some of them into an electric skillet, but they were still round.

I noticed, after a while, that she was leaving them round. I said, "Gene, when are you going to flatten them?"

Apparently, Gene had not realized that they needed to be flat.

She joked, "Oh, I didn't want them to be like the small ones at Burger King!"

She took the spatula and flattened the burgers.

We really enjoyed the final results.

After we ate our hamburgers and drank cokes, Pam and Gary played pool in the recreation room near the pool. Then we all headed to the beach to throw a beachball around.

Gene decided that we should walk to the Oceanus where the Gamma would be docking soon. We all walked from the Groves' home down the beach, to the dock.

When the Gamma arrived, we joked to Mr. and Mrs. Groves, asking if they had "re-entry" permits to the Island!

Chapter Thirty-nine

Golden

It was late afternoon and the sun was low in the sky. My sisters, Carole, Pamela, Brenda and I were walking at Silver Cove as the setting sun slowly painted a golden glow on all of us.

As we walked along the water's soft edge, the water and the sand also turned golden. Then our skin turned as gold as the girl in "Gold Finger."

The sun highlighted our dark hair in gold, almost as thick as gold leaf. Brenda's hazel-green eyes turned to golden hazel under dark eyelashes tipped in gold.

I turned to my sisters and exclaimed, "Oh *why* don't I have a camera, we are golden! We are *golden!*"

Carole said, "Look at the water!"

The soft gilded underbellies of the clouds were reflecting gold onto the water. It looked as if golden silk were floating on the water and the sun, glistening off of it, filled the very air with a Midas glow….

Chapter Forty

Tickets to the horse show

Pinetree Stables was going to have their yearly horseshow.

Gene, Brenda, and I rode through neighborhoods selling tickets to the show. Gene rode Sandy Man, I rode Delilah, and Brenda rode Delilah's dam, Bahama Mama. We canvassed neighborhoods, knocking on doors to sell tickets. After about an hour, we were near the Groves' mansion on the beach.

The Hayward mansion is just to the left of the Groves, so we decided to knock on their door.

As we approached the Hayward home, their Rhodesian Ridgeback dogs ran towards us. Not good. These dogs are large, dark tan dogs that have a stripe of hair that grows forward down their backs. Hair that stands up, creating a "small ridge." The dogs originated in Africa, where they were used to hunt lions. Now they were hunting us.

One dog leapt almost as high as the top of the horse's rumps, snapping and barking as we approached the front door.

Despite the commotion, no one came to the door, so we decided to leave. We didn't want to stir the dogs up any more.

As we turned to leave, Gene said, "Let's have lunch at my house! Victoria always has something prepared."

"Great!"

Hungry, we rode next door to the Groves' home.

At the house, we put the horses in a grassy area which was shaded by mimosa trees. Gene unsaddled Sandy Man, as Brenda snapped a photo of her. Brenda also unsaddled Mama. I had ridden Delilah bareback, so I didn't have to unsaddle her. I left her to graze with the other horses while we ate lunch.

As we walked into the arboretum, the green, tropical plants created a cool entrance even as the sun shone upon them. We went into the house and Gene led us to the right, where we took a few steps down the gleaming marble steps into the large living room.

There was a grand piano to our left, and a comfortable seating area and television in the middle of the room. The furniture was arranged in the center of the room on a huge Tabriz rug.

I later learned this rug was made in the late 19th century and is a copy of a 16th century Persian design. Mr. Groves had purchased it from his sister around 1961.

The back wall of the living room is made up of doors that open to the tropical backyard and to the beach just beyond. There are a few tall coconut palm trees and a gate just before you reach the beach.

One time I accidentally tripped the alarm in this area and the maid, Victoria, came running and turned the alarm off.

We walked past the living room, towards the dining room. There is a tall, carved wooden divider that separates the living and dining area. On the other side of it, is a huge, antique dining room table that looks like it came from a castle. There is also is a foot buzzer to summon servants when needed.

Gene turned right again, and we followed her into a long room just before the kitchen. It was the Butler's pantry.

Gene said, "Choose a tray to put your lunch on." She pointed to a lower cabinet that had dozens of slots in it. Each slot had different trays. Some were silver and others were wood. We each took a tray and continued into the kitchen. Gene uncovered a bowl of orange sections and a plate of sandwiches. We put some onto our trays and went outside to eat under the trees where the horses grazed.

After we finished lunch, Gene said, "Let's ride on the beach!"

"Okay!" Brenda and I replied in unison.

Gene went into the large pool house nearby and changed into a yellow bikini. She said, "Don't forget, we always have guest bathing suits in the pool house."

Brenda put on a red one-piece bathing suit, and I chose a similar one in black.

We rode the horses bareback across the sand dunes to the beach. When we reached the beach, Delilah started pawing at the water's edge, splashing water all around her. Suddenly, she tucked her legs under her and lay down in the surf, relishing the refreshing water.

Brenda took photos of the moment, but, in the excitement, she forgot to advance the film!

"Take a picture of me and Sandy!" Gene said.

155

"Okay, Gene! Stand in front of your house!"

Gene led Sandy Man to where the Groves' mansion and palm trees were in the background. Sandy was wet and shiny from being in the ocean.

As I readied the camera, Sandy Man suddenly lay down in the soft white sand. Gene looked at him in surprise, and just before he actually rolled, I took the photo.

We all laughed as he rolled in the sand.

He truly became a Sandy Man!

Chapter Forty-one

The Horse Show

Brenda and I decided to enter Delilah into the "Fancy Dress" Contest at the horseshow. She was going as a "flower child."

We gathered purple bougainvillea flowers everywhere we could find them. We painstakingly attached flower after flower to Delilah's saddle blanket careful to leave room with no flowers where the saddle would sit.

We also found some yellow lace from an old bridesmaid dress and used it to cover Delilah's saddle.

Brenda took some lavender ribbon and wrapped the bridle leather with it.

Once the saddle blanket, saddle, and bridle had been converted to a fairytale look, we made small bougainvillea bouquets to go in Delilah's mane, and also made a flower bracelet for her right pastern.

We worked late into the night preparing everything and decided Brenda would ride Delilah in the show.

The next day, we went to the stable and washed Delilah, and

outfitted her in her flower-adorned saddle and beribboned bridle.

There was a small black mare named Daiquiri, whose rider was disguised as the Headless Horseman.

Daiquiri was a Paso Fino, and her quick, choppy leg movements, black color, and headless rider absolutely won the class. The Blue ribbon!

Brenda and I were a little disappointed but knew the entire class of entries had been bested by Daiquiri's spooky, impressive showing.

As we went to remove Delilah's flowery tack, suddenly Marion M dressed as a Russian Cossack, came to us. She had won a white ribbon riding Lady Willpower.

Marion held out her ribbon and tried to give it to us. She thought we had done such a pretty job on Delilah, that she wanted us to have *her* ribbon.

Of course, we didn't accept it, but how kind of Marion M.

Marion wasn't the only gallant one that day.

We had noticed that one of the horses, a brown gelding, named Chocolate Jim was standing in his stall in a pool of blood so deep, hay was floating in it.

Somehow, he had cut a tiny vein in his face, and, fortunately, Dr. Robert was at the show.

Dr. Robert went into the stall and sewed up the tiny but dangerous wound.

Chocolate Jim recovered.

Chapter Forty-two

Horses escape

Delilah was assigned to the first stall on the left in the first row of stalls at Pinetree Stables. All of the horses were allowed out during the day to graze in the pastures. One afternoon, Myra's husband, Brian frantically rushed up to me and said, "The horses are out! And Delilah is one of them!"

"Oh, she is?" I calmly replied.

I saw the small band of horses whipping about like a small school of fish. Delilah's size made her easy to see in the herd and I whistled for her.

Delilah broke from the excited group and pranced over to me. Brian looked astonished as he asked, "How did you get her to come to you like that?"

I replied, "The first thing I taught her is to come to me. She can be bribed."

I was only kidding; by now I had learned that Delilah loved me as much as I loved her. We had become so bonded that I could put her anywhere, untied, and know that she would stay with me, or come to me. I patted her, and we walked to the safety of her stall.

Chapter Forty-three

Freeport News Plane.

Delilah was big and could easily hold two riders. One day, my younger sister, Pamela and I rode double on her to Silver Cove.

As Delilah high-stepped down the beach, we noticed a red Freeport News airplane circling above us.

We didn't know that they were filming us.

Later a friend said she had seen the clip of us riding Delilah that day. It was shown at the Columbus Movie Theatre.

She said, the film ended with the camera zooming in on Delilah's front legs as she was beating a rhythm in the sand of Silver Cove.

Chapter Forty-four

Going to England

Mr. and Mrs. Groves owned an estate in England, called Lyneham House. The large, stone, manor house is over four-hundred years old, and has more than six hundred acres surrounding it. It is located in southern England, near Plymouth.

Gene and Gayle would spend the summer riding some of the Lyneham horses in horse shows and Gene invited Brenda and me to come visit.

I would go to England first, and Brenda would go to England when I returned to Freeport.

I got all of my tickets and caught a flight out of Freeport to England, with stops in Miami and New York.

My trip was going well, until I got to New York. I noticed I was missing my ticket to London! I had no idea if it had been stolen or what. It was gone!

Fortunately, we have some friends, the Amsels, in New York. I called Robyn Amsel, and her mother offered to let me stay the night with them, until I could catch another flight the following day.

Brenda and I had met Robyn and her family when they were vacationing in Freeport. The family was eating dinner at the Captain's Chart House which is located just off of Sunrise Highway. We had to ride past the restaurant anytime we rode the horses to the beach. One afternoon, Brenda was riding Lady Willpower past the Chart House. Suddenly, a girl of about eighteen, came running towards her. It was Robyn Amsel. Robyn was so excited about the gorgeous mare, that she fled her steak dinner to come pet Lady.

Brenda invited the Amsels to come to our home later that evening, and Robyn ended up spending a few days with us.

Robyn and her Mom picked me up at the airport so that I could spend the night at their house, and they would return me to the airport the following day. In the meantime, I sent a telegram to Gene to let her know that I would be a day late arriving. I was disappointed that the delay would cause me to miss the famous Hickstead Horse Show.

Robyn and I caught up on what was going on with her, and what the latest news was from Freeport. The next morning, Mrs.

Amsel made us a great breakfast of omelets and bagels. After we ate, Robyn and I rode yellow bicycles to a drug store for some makeup. We also went to a nearby stable. None of the horses were as beautiful as Delilah.

When we returned to Robyn's house, we ate some brownies and I hurriedly gathered my belongings for the flight to London.

Robyn is so nice. She gave me a black blouse with ruffles on it to wear in England. She also gave me a Paul McCartney album, and a beaded necklace with a peace sign on it.

Mrs. Amsel and Robyn drove me to the airport and waited with me for the 7:00 PM Pan Am to London. Mrs. Amsel kindly gave me a little pocket money, knowing I had to spend most of my cash to replace my lost ticket.

Thanks to Mom's friend, Mr. Reynolds, my ticket was upgraded to First-Class.

Once I boarded the plane, I sat next to a young man, Mr. Guinness, who lives in Puerto Rico. After dinner, he slept. Nighttime seemed only about an hour long. After we were served a small breakfast, we landed at Heathrow at about 7:00 AM.

After Customs, I stepped out into the chilly weather and hailed a taxi to Reading station where I bought a railroad ticket to Plymouth on the 10:25 AM train.

Once I boarded the train, I sat across from an elderly man and woman. I found it charming how the old man's face would droop like a hound dog as he looked down at his newspaper, yet when he looked at his wife, his entire face and forehead would shift dramatically upwards.

People bring their own food onto these trains and I watched as his wife unwrapped some sandwiches for them.

After a few hours, the train arrived in Yealmpton.

Although I had sent several telegrams to Gene about my delay, I sent another telegram to Lyneham House from the small Yealmpton Post Office. I asked the Post Mistress about taxis and was directed to talk to a man at Hendricks' garage next door.

I asked the owner, Mr. Hendricks, how I could get a cab. He said, "Yealmpton is too small to have a cab company, but I will be happy to drive you to Lyneham. I used to work there."

"Thank you, Mr. Hendricks."

He opened the 'boot' of his car and put my suitcase into it. Then he walked around to the left side of the car and opened the passenger door for me. We drove just a few minutes until we reached two towering gates. Mr. Hendricks drove through the gates, that, frankly, made me think of the Pearly Gates. We continued down a long drive to the 400-year-old manor house.

There was a circular, gravel driveway and Mr. Hendricks parked at the entrance to the home.

"How much do I owe you, Mr. Hendricks?"

"I wouldn't think of it, Miss. It was my pleasure." he said as he set my suitcase at the front door.

"Oh, Thank you Mr. Hendricks. I really appreciate your help!" He smiled and turned to his car as I clanged on the door with the heavy, stag-head shaped door knocker.

My knock was answered by a female servant. "Hello, you must be Linda Smith, I'm Velma, Mr. Groves is expecting you." She showed me to a large library, just to the left of the foyer.

Mr. Groves sat behind a huge desk in the wood-paneled room. He stood up smiling and said, "Welcome Miss Smith, I hope you had no trouble finding us." "No, Mr. Groves, I had great help from Mr. Hendricks at Hendricks Garage. He drove me here." Mr. Groves replied, "It was good of Mr. Hendricks to help you. Have a seat, dear," he said as he gestured to a plush chair in front of his desk. As I sat down, he pointed out a spindle on his desk. "I received your telegrams."

The spindle had the telegrams I had sent at each stage of my journey, most likely starting with the one where I would be delayed when I lost my plane ticket. Mr. Groves knew that I had to buy another ticket. He kindly said, "Dear, do you need any money?"

Although I had very limited funds for the rest of my trip, I replied, "No thank you."

Mr. Groves said, "Let me show you the gardens." As we left the library, the servant was about to head up the massive dark wooden staircase with my suitcase in hand.

Mr. Groves addressed her, "Velma, we will be in the garden. When we return, please show Miss Smith to her room. She may want to rest before dinner."

The two of us, he, an aristocratic entrepreneur of about seventy, and me, a young woman of twenty, walked outside where the large gravel drive meets the house. We turned left and walked down a path to an antique garden where some of the stone walls had crumbled over time.

Despite the crumbling walls, the garden was lush and well-tended. One area had raspberries growing profusely. Big, fat red-pink raspberries. Mr. Groves picked a handful of raspberries and held his hand out and placed them into mine. I looked at the ruby jewels in my hand and popped a couple of them into my mouth. They were as sweet as candy.

" These are delicious, thank you! "

"You are welcome." he replied. We leisurely walked in the garden while Mr. Groves told me about Lyneham. He said, "Lyneham House is 650 acres 90 acres of which are planted in white clover pastures." We have farmers that raise sheep here." He also said there were very old oak trees and vast fields.

We came to a large swimming pool adjacent to the garden.

Mr. Groves pointed out a building near the pool which he called the "Orangerie." He explained that these huge manor houses had this type of building similar to a greenhouse, where they would grow fruits and other vegetables during the cold, foggy months of winter.

In a few minutes, one of Gene's younger brothers, Graham, joined us.

"Hi, Linda," he said with a grin. "Hi Graham!" I responded.

The three of us continued to walk. Although Graham was only about twelve years old, Mr. Groves started talking to him about business. "Graham, do you know what an entrepreneur' is?"

Graham didn't know, but Mr. Groves did and went on to explain a bit of it to Graham.

A few minutes later, Mr. Groves asked me "Dear, would you like to see the stables? The walk is a bit long for me, but Graham will show you."

"Yes, I would love that!" I replied. "Thank you for the tour and the raspberries!" "My pleasure." he replied.

Mr. Groves turned to walk back to the house as Graham and I continued down a white gravel path towards the stable. We spied a little bay horse. Graham said, "Some of the farmers horses wander onto our property." He chased it into a different pasture.

We came to a forest that looked as if it were Sherwood Forest. The trees were enormous, yet there were vast, clear spaces under the trees where you could easily race a horse through.

"Wow, Graham, do you think we will run into Robin Hood?"

He laughed.

When we arrived at the stable, it was quiet. The employees and several of the horses were still on their return trip from London with Gene, Gayle and Mrs. Groves.

The stable is likely four-hundred years old and is made of stone like the manor house. There are two rows of stalls facing each other.

Graham said, "I just wanted to show you where the stable is, we won't stay long. You probably need a break from your trip."

"Thanks, Graham, I do."

We headed back to the house.

Chapter Forty-five

Spooked

Velma, the maid, met us as we came in. She said, "I put your suitcase upstairs, Miss. May I show you to your room? It is on the right at the top of the stairs just past the bathroom."

I replied, "Thank you, I can find it. I think I will rest awhile before Gene returns from London."

As I walked up the massive stairway to the fourth floor, I suddenly felt a sense of apprehension.

On the fourth floor, I turned right down a short hall. There was a bathroom on the left, and just past it, the room I would be sharing with Gene. I entered the room and saw a large mahogany bed just to my left. I assumed that was Gene's bed.

There was a large casement window with tall shutters on the opposite side of her bed. My suitcase was on a smaller bed that was a dozen feet or so from the foot of Gene's bed. My bed was at a right angle to her bed.

The roof slanted slightly over my bed. I could see the wallpaper was a soft cream color, with light green scenes of sheep grazing.

After removing some clothes from my suitcase, I headed down the hall to take a bath.

The bathroom is long and narrow with a claw-foot tub on the right, and a sink and counter on the left. The door is a heavy wooden door with a skeleton key in it, and at the far end of the room there is a gable-window. As I drew my bath, I still couldn't shake the feeling of apprehension.

As I slipped into the warm, soothing water, I felt as if I were being watched.

As I finished my bath, my hand flew to my neck as I suddenly realized I was not wearing my St. Christopher medal. I had worn it continuously for more than two years of travel never taking it off even for baths. At the same instant, I saw the St. Christopher medal lying on the counter next to the sink.

When had I removed it? I quickly stepped out of the tub and reached for it, still feeling as if I were being watched…

I quickly grabbed a towel, dressed and turned the skeleton key to unlock the bathroom door. Nothing happened. I tried again and again, to no avail. The bathroom was on the fourth floor and I knew no one was likely to hear me. I tried the key several more times, and, to my relief, the door finally opened!

I must need some rest, I thought. I lay down and dozed for a couple of hours.

I awoke to the sound of Gene laughing as she said, "Hi, it's about time you got here. I hope you got some rest!"

"Thanks Gene, I did! How was the horse show? I hate I missed it!" Gene replied, "We did great! Grayling VI and Bengal Tiger won 13 rosettes!"

"Oh, I *Love* their names!" I exclaimed. Gene said, "We love them too, but they are the stable's show horses. Dad has promised to get us horses of our own."

"Wow! How exciting!" I exclaimed.

Gene said, "I think I will take a bath and get ready for dinner. It is at 7:30 sharp." Gene headed down the hall to take a bath.

I didn't mention trapping myself in the bathroom.

Chapter Forty-six

Beds

Gene and I went downstairs to the first floor where she showed me to the huge den where we would eat.

There is a long dining table to the left as we entered the huge, dark-wood paneled room. At the end of the table is a large sideboard where a couple of silver trays held teapots.

At the opposite end of the den there are several casement windows. The windows are set high and the afternoon sun streamed in.

To the right of the entrance is a large royal blue sofa which is situated directly in front of a huge stone fireplace. The tables on either end of the sofa have silver bowls full of red raspberries.

Flames from the fire reflected in the silver bowls and made the heavy wood panels cast a warm glow in the room.

There were several comfortable seating areas with game tables in the room as well.

Gene's younger siblings, Gayle, Graham and Gary were already seated at the dining table and we joined them.

Both Gary and Gayle greeted me, just as Mr. and Mrs. Groves came in.

Georgette Groves greeted me warmly, "Welcome, Linda, we are happy you made it!"

"Thank you for having me!" I replied.

Mr. Groves was happy to have the girls back from the Horse Show and decided to play a joke on them.

He said, "Girls, I finally got the horses you wanted!"

Gene and Gayle were very excited.

He said, "They are in the pasture nearest the house, we'll see them after we eat!"

After dinner, Gene, Gayle, and I quickly followed Mr. Groves out to the pasture. There were indeed a couple of horses. Not the new show horses for the girls, but a couple of nags that had wandered onto the estate.

Mr. Groves laughed as he introduced the girls to their "new" horses. Gayle and Gene were very dismayed. I was caught in between.

I enjoyed Mr. Groves' lighthearted sense of humor!

The next morning, frankly, I didn't know if I should make my bed or leave it for the servants. In such extraordinary surroundings with servants everywhere, I wasn't sure if I would look foolish for making my bed.

Gene had not made her bed.

Well, when in doubt, always follow the lead of your host. Gene didn't make her bed, and neither did I.

It didn't take long for Georgette to corner both of us on our way to breakfast. She chastised us for not making our beds!

I apologized and stuttered that I was not sure what to do, so I followed Gene's lead!

Drat! I had not meant to blame Gene!

Chapter Forty-seven

Gene makes Islands in stream.

As we walked back to Lyneham Gene said, "Let's hurry, I want to help make lunch. I never get to cook!"

Gene was very interested in learning to cook, but, because they had cooks in all of their homes, Gene rarely got to experiment in the kitchen. When she did, she really put her heart into it.

I remember one time in Freeport she tried a recipe for "Islands in the Stream."

The main part of the dessert is basically meringue, so the recipe calls for a lot of egg whites.

I went into the kitchen where Gene had two or three dozen eggs she was using to create her masterpiece.

She carefully separated the egg whites from the yellow and whipped the egg whites into meringue. Then she carefully floated poofs of meringue on top of a custard that had a tinge of blue food dye to represent the ocean.

When Gene presented the delicate dessert at the dinner table, Mr. and Mrs. Groves started naming the "Islands."

"This is New Providence, this is Long Island, this is Grand Bahama…"

The islands actually tasted good.

Especially Grand Bahama!

When we returned to the manor house, Gene was disappointed that lunch was ready.

"Oh well, Gene said, "Dad's Secretary, Tom Rossack will arrive tomorrow from Freeport. Maybe I can make something when he gets here."

Chapter Forty-eight

Picking Raspberries

The horses have a day off today, so Gene, Gayle and I decided to pick raspberries and walk the young golden labs.

The two puppies are almost grown and love exploring the vast estate with us. We three girls walked in a huge field which is planted in white clover as the half-grown pups ran and explored nearby.

Friendly bees bumbled about the clover as Gene took photos.

After a few shots she said, "Let's go to the lanes and find some berries."

Gene knew huge bowers of raspberries spilled over the fences along the lane and had brought a container with us for berries.

After leaving the field of clover, we trekked through more of the Robin Hood forests and exited onto one of the many lanes.

Gene said, "We will see Graham soon. He is helping Mr. Hodges trim some of the hedges along the lane. Land owners are responsible for keeping the lanes clear as the lanes are sometimes used by the public."

Linda - Lynham Estate, ENGLAND

Just as she finished the sentence, we ran into Graham and Mr. Hodges. After greeting them, we left them to work in earnest.

We found a bower of raspberries to raid. After picking some of the delightful fruit, I said, "Gene, I have a welt on my arm." Gene took a look at the small mark and pulled a green leaf from a vine.

She said, "Here, this will fix it, this is a medicine leaf." I took the small green leaf and rubbed it on the mark. The welt went away almost instantly. I was impressed and exclaimed, "Thanks, Gene, you should be a doctor!"

As we continued picking raspberries, we heard an approaching car sound its horn just around the corner. The corners are blind, and although there is very little traffic, the rule is to sound your horn as you approach each blind curve. A black car came into view, with two men inside.
I recognized Mr. Groves' Secretary, Tom Rossack. There was a handsome young blond man in the passenger seat. Tom's partner.

Tom rolled down the window and greeted us. He said, "May I present C." The young man replied, "How do you do?"

He had a German accent.

Gene said, "Nice to meet you C. Tom, just continue down the lane, you can't miss the house. Mom and Dad are expecting you."

C? Suddenly I realized this darling young man is the same German that I met at the stable in Freeport. The one that could not take the bridle off of his horse.

Chapter Forty-nine

Let's Ride

Gene and I finished breakfast but waited for Mr. and Mrs. Groves to come down to eat. We would be going riding with Tom and C, so, although we left the breakfast table, we made ourselves comfortable on the nearby sofas. The Groves came down followed a few minutes later by Tom and C.

Gene worked on a needle-point, while I sat dreamily in front of the fireplace. I could hear Mr. Groves talking business to Tom Rossack, while Mrs. Groves talked to C about the gardens.

When they finished breakfast, Gene, Gayle, Tom, C, and I went to the stable.

Once at the stable, I could see for myself how beautiful the big grey, Grayling VI was and how black and muscular Bengal Tiger was. Grayling is a huge grey horse with big grey circles of dapples on his rump and sides. He has a very thick white tail that touches the ground.

Bengal Tiger is black with a long lean look to him. He looks sinewy with fine muscles like a sleek feline predator. He looks more like a black leopard rather than a Bengal Tiger.

Anna, one of the stable girls, asked me how much riding experience I had.

I said, "I own a mare, and I like a spirited horse."

She pointed out two horses and said, "Restari is a good horse and easy to handle. Martin is a lot more spirited but will settle down. Either can be ridden with an English saddle or a Western saddle."

"I will ride Martin, and since I'm in England, I will ride English!"

Gayle rode Shammy, and Gene rode Philippa's horse, Shamrock Lad. Tom and C rode Rosa and Restari.

We rode through long, peaceful lanes to a vast pasture that looked like miles of lush green grass, and wide-open spaces. We were all relaxed and chatted about the horse show. Rosa and Restari were very placid and well-behaved.

Martin was not placid at all. He was almost in a frenzy as some flies were biting him on his face and buzzing around his ears.

When we reached a huge field, he started rearing and running sideways in a mad attempt to escape the flies.

By now the other riders were well ahead of me and I was afraid Martin would fall from running sideways downhill.

I firmly tapped the downhill side of his neck, hoping to urge him to go forward, rather than sideways. It worked and we raced across the field.

The others were waiting for me with worried looks on their faces. As I rode up to them, with Martin finally under control, I was grinning, and exclaimed, "That was the *best* ride ever!"

Martin settled down, and we all continued to ride through the magnificent forests and fields of clover. It was an exhilarating ride every step of the way!

When we returned to the stable, the girls there took care of the horses.

I looked inside one of the stalls. The walls were stone and there was a very large trough made of stone.

One of the stable girls brought in a metal bucket filled with water. She told me that the horses were given water separately from their meals.

"We think their grain will swell when a horse drinks water, so we give them water well before we feed them." she said.

The next morning at breakfast, C sat to my left. He seemed as vulnerable as he had been at the stable when he was unsure as to how one removes a horse's bridle.

Mr. Groves spoke kindly to him, "Would you care for tea, C?"

"Ya, thank you."

C stood up and leaned forward with his china cup as Mr. Groves poured steaming tea into the cup.

C was one of the most handsome men I had ever seen.

I think we girls were disappointed that he was going to leave after breakfast.

Later in the day, Gene and I were in a huge downstairs laundry room. I was getting my clothes out of the dryer and Gene was doing some ironing. (Georgette always made certain that her children knew how to do chores, despite all of the servants available to them).

C came in and formally bid us farewell. He was leaving Lyneham for London.

We hated to see him go.

Chapter Fifty

Squab

The main course for dinner tonight is squab. Squab is a young pigeon that has not yet grown feathers.

One of the kitchen staff carefully placed a small, bloody, bird onto each of our plates.

I stared at my plate then cast a furtive look at the rest of the Groves' children. They were all frozen staring at their plates.

After a moment, they all started grumbling.

The cook was summoned and she asked what was wrong.

We chimed in that we wanted the birds cooked a little longer. The cook retreated to the kitchen with the small flock of birds.

In a few minutes, she returned to the table with them.

Still rare.

I could practically see my little bird's heart throbbing under its small breast as thin blood seeped onto my plate. Once again, the plates were sent back to the kitchen.

This time, Gene and I marched along with them to explain that the birds needed to be "cooked."

For a third time, they were brought to the table, still rare.

Mr. Groves graciously thanked the cook and had her remove the birds. The cook brought out a large baron of beef and placed it on the sideboard where Mr. Groves carved it and served us all roast beef.

This is how I learned that the Brits always serve squab rare. The cook truly thought she would ruin it if it were cooked through.

Chapter Fifty-one

Disembodied Presence

My bed is about twelve feet from Gene's bed, and sideways to hers and I can only see her footboard from my bed.

Gene can't see me when she is in bed, not only because her footboard blocks her view of my bed, but she has a habit of wearing a black-silk sleeping mask like the glamorous movie stars used to wear.

I wished Gene could see me from her bed, because I continued to feel a little spooked when I'm upstairs.

I think one reason is that there is a wooden trap door a couple of feet from my bed.

It is a fire escape.

If you open the trap door, there is a ladder attached to the wall which you would use to climb down one floor. On the next floor, there is another trap door which leads down to another floor. The fire escape continues to the main floor.

As I started to close my eyes, I felt a *presence* just to the right side of my face.

Close.

I had a strong sense that if I were to let myself drift off to sleep, the presence would *speak* to me.

In order to remain awake, I focused on the sheep in the wallpaper, and started, well, counting sheep. Is this where people learned to count sheep, I wondered.

I would count fast to keep my mind occupied and not let the disembodied voice intrude.

I was trying to be a good guest, so I didn't mention this to Gene.

A few nights later, I was beginning to relax.

Finally.

There was a breeze coming in the large casement window next to Gene's bed. The shutters were open, and every now and then, a gust of wind caused them to make a banging noise.

On top of that, the moon was full and shone brightly into the room.

Gene had her dark mask on and mumbled something about the sound.

I was awake, and said, "Gene, I can take care of that."

Gene peeked one eye out from under her mask and said, "Thanks, Linda, I am so tired."

"No problem." I replied.

I walked around her bed and stood in front of the huge window. I grasped the shutter handles while looking out at a very moonlit night.

The wind stopped.

I blinked a couple of times as I realized there was a man standing on the path below.

The man was dressed in clothing from another century and had long white hair like a pilgrim. He was wearing a coat that came half-way down the calves of his legs.

I could see through him.

A smile came to my face, as I felt he was communicating with me. I fully realized, almost telepathically, that he was telling me, *"See, you recognized for days that I was here. I am showing myself to you at a distance that wouldn't frighten you."*

I felt very calm, yet I was desperate for Gene to see him. I didn't want to tell her what I was seeing-I had to make her get up and look for herself.

I kept saying, "Gene, you have to get up and look at the moonlight. You won't believe it."

She mumbled, turned over, and ignored my urgings.

The next morning, I explained to Gene about what I saw. She told her mother.

"There are NO such things as ghosts!!" Mrs. Groves said.

There I was, the uncouth fool who let her ignorant mind run away with her.

However, later that day at the stable, Gene blurted my story out to the stable girls.

One of the girls replied, "Oh, that is the ghost at the pump house. We have all seen him!"

I was never afraid in the house again.

Chapter Fifty-two

Journey's End Pub

One night, the Groves decided we would all go to Plymouth and have dinner. Mr. and Mrs. Groves as well as: Gene, Graham, Gayle, Gary, Tom Rossack, and I got into two black Bentleys.

Tom drove one car with several of us in it and followed Mr. Groves who was driving the first car.

We came to a centuries-old building called 'Journey's End.' The quaint restaurant had small doors to accommodate the smaller people of the past and the building is perched right on the edge of a steep cliff that overlooks the ocean.

Someone mentioned that this building had been here since the 13th century.

We crowded into a tiny bar that had barrels as tables.

There was a large wheel of a white cheese on the bar.

It is called Stilton cheese.

I didn't know what to order as an aperitif, so I looked to Gene to see what she would order. Gene asked for a Dubonnet.

I did the same.

Dubonnet was a sweet, thick and fruity drink that paired well with the salty Stilton cheese and crackers.

After our before- dinner drink, we all gathered around a long, narrow table and enjoyed a dinner of roast beef, potatoes and

Yorkshire pudding.

L to R. Secretary Tom Rossack , Wallace Groves, Graham Groves, Gayle Groves. Back right is Gary Groves, Georgette Groves, and Linda Smith.

Chapter Fifty-three

The Bird Cage

One day Georgette sent Gene and me to Plymouth to pick up a couple of items she had an Antique shop hold for her.

Mrs. Groves didn't carry cash, so she often had items holding at different stores for her. We went into the Antique shop and Gene paid for the choice items.

The bird cage was exquisite. It was made of silver and had red stained-glass along the lower sides of it.

There was a lovely silver heart-shaped mirror as well.

Mrs. Groves always struck me as a romantic person, and her choice of the mirror only deepened that impression of her.

After we picked up the silver purchases, we went to a nearby pet store where Gene bought a beautiful yellow and black canary. She also bought birdseed and we returned to Lyneham House.

Mrs. Groves was delighted with the canary. She put it and its food into the bird cage and hung the cage at the far end of the den.

Speaking of the Groves being romantic, there is a photo that is in the Groves' penthouse in Freeport.

It was taken at a social gathering such as a cocktail party.

Mr. and Mrs. Groves are not standing very close to each other yet a photographer captured a glance between Wallace and Georgette Groves that clearly shows the bond between them.

That momentary glance of two people that are lovers, confidants, partners, and soul mates.

Chapter Fifty-four

Staircase

Brenda's notes:

One day as I climbed the stairway to the third floor of Lyneham House, I came to a landing with an open door to my left. I had never paid attention to the door before as it was always closed.

Today, it was open.

I was drawn to see what lay beyond, so I walked through the door.

Once through, I found myself on the landing of another staircase, a staircase that ran parallel to the one I had been using to go upstairs.

This staircase was particularly luxurious, compared to the one I had just left.

It was lighted with sparkling chandeliers. The carpet was incredibly plush and gold-framed oil paintings hung on the walls of the staircase.

I had always appreciated fine art, and I was drawn to the paintings. I had to slowly descend the stairs a step at a time and pause to study them.

One stood out as it was a pen and ink drawing rather than an oil painting. The drawing depicted an English village.

There were little shops lining a main street, with people and dogs as well as horse carts. At the end of the main street stood a massive stone house.

I suddenly recognized the house at the end of the street, the house that towered over all of the others. It was the house I was standing in - Lyneham House!

I was immediately aware of how Lyneham House wasn't just a house. It was a home, built to last for generations, and indeed had survived several centuries.

The town over which it presided, had since crumbled into oblivion, swallowed up by forests.

Now I knew why, when riding one of the English thoroughbreds through the woods, I would see the edge of a stone well, or other stone structures on the sides of the riding path.

This regal staircase may have been used for visiting Royalty, and I assumed the other stairway, as nice as it was, had been used for children and servants.

Chapter Fifty-five

Belle Nuit

Brenda's notes:

Linda had missed the Hickstead Horseshow on her visit, but I was in luck as there was another horseshow coming up, one that Gene and Gayle would also ride in. It was located near Lyneham House.

The day before the show, Gene and I shopped for equestrian attire. As I was looking at equestrian clothes, one of my favorite songs by the Beatles called "Something" came on.

At the horseshow, while Gene and Gayle prepared for their own classes, Mr. Groves and I strolled past a class of fine show horses.

Mr. Groves asked, "Which one do you think will win, my dear?"

I was flattered that he wanted my opinion.

I had always loved horses and I studied the group.

One horse stood out.

Her name was 'Belle Nuit' which means Beautiful Night in French.

I said to Mr. Groves, "I like the black, the one with the white star."

We stopped and watched the judges decide, and, after a few minutes, a judge named Belle Nuit as the First- Place winner and attached a big blue rosette onto her bridle.

All of those years reading horse stories and looking at horse pictures had taught me something after all!

Chapter Fifty-six

Swan Lake

Brenda's notes:

I also had the drama of riding the fractious horse, Martin.

One afternoon as I galloped Martin across the deep green fields of Lyneham estate, I turned him towards a dam, situated between two lakes. I couldn't resist the appeal of dashing across the wide, grass- covered dam.

One side of the dam had a lake, and the other side had a steep incline that acted as a spillway for the lake.

As Martin and I flew across the dam, a huge male swan suddenly arose from the deep grass by the edge of the lake and charged towards us.

The drake flapped his large wings and snaked his head at us, in a threatening move.

Martin was startled and immediately leapt sideways a couple of times. I was sure that we would fall over the steep side of the dam! However, he quickly regained his forward movement and we soon outran the danger.

Chapter Fifty-seven

Leaving Lyneham House

Time for me to head back to the Bahamas. Gene and I seized the day and took a short early ride before I packed for my departure.

I thanked the entire Groves' family and Gene drove me to the 6:30 pm train to London.

The train trip to London takes about four hours, and I arrived in London about 10:30 pm. I stayed in a small hotel near the airport and returned to the airport early the next morning.

After I ate breakfast, I caught the morning 747 Pan Am to New York.

No need to hurry. Not only was the flight an hour late departing, but the movie and stereo system had conked out.

The highlight of the flight was when I saw some icebergs off the coast of Newfoundland.

We finally landed in New York at 1:45 pm.

After going through Customs, I took the bus to the Eastern Airlines Terminal and called Robyn and her family before catching the 4 pm EAL to Miami. I wanted to thank them again for helping me on the first day of my journey.

The First Class Eastern Airline flight was very nice.

In Miami, I boarded the last flight of my trip at 7:55 pm to Freeport.

Customs was easy as usual. The Custom Agents are very friendly and have never given us any trouble. Not even the time I brought a deep-dish Key Lime pie from Miami.

The Bahamian agent joked that he really needed to cut it to see if anything was in it, meaning he wanted a piece.

The Bahamians are always so pleasant and cheerful.

Mom, Pam, and Brenda picked me up at the airport as I raved about the great trip.

Brenda had bad news, though. She told me that Gene's little horse, Sandy Man, had escaped from a tourist on Friday and was struck by a taxi on Sunrise Highway! He was killed instantly!

Gene will be heartbroken.

Chapter Fifty-eight

Air Traffic Control Freeport

A.R. Smith, the Chief of Air Traffic Control in Freeport, said, "When a pilot is lost, the hardest part is to convince the pilot that he must pay attention to his instruments."

"I had a lost pilot that had departed Florida on his way to Walker Cay."

The FAA was trying to assist the pilot and get an aircraft up with a directional finder, but he was too low for radar."

"I *reckoned* he had to be on the Walker Cay side of Grand Bahama. Since he wouldn't use his instruments, I was trying to get him to navigate by the sun, but he was in and out of clouds."

"I told him to keep the sun off of his left wing and he was just a few minutes off of Grand Bahama. I also scrambled another pilot to try and locate the lost plane."

"Other pilots listened in."

"I could hear the sound of the pilot's passengers screaming in the background."

"The search pilot saw the lost plane just as it neared Grand Bahama. The pilot was almost hysterical by the time he landed at West End. Everyone on the plane was upset, but, fortunately, survived."

Daddy told me about another incident that occurred when a company pilot for a company I will leave unnamed flew from Miami, to Freeport one evening. The pilot had flown company executives to a meeting in Miami and decided to take the corporate jet on a quick trip to Freeport. He was accompanied by a woman who was not his wife.

As he approached Freeport, the plane was too low and hit the water. Another airline pilot saw a flash and reported to the tower that he thought a plane had gone down.

Search and Rescue responded. It took several hours to find the pilot.

He was found just before daylight, clinging to a seat cushion. He had been partially scalped and had a broken leg.

The woman's body was never recovered.

The company he worked for actually had him sign an agreement that *he* would not sue *them*.

Another time, a wealthy man was missing and ATC dispatched planes to search for him. He was finally found when a diver looked under the man's yacht, and found the man drowned with an anchor chain around his neck.

This death was deemed an accident.

The gift shop at the airport was a bustling place for travelers seeking gifts to take back to the U.S. We saw many movie stars and other famous people in the shop over time.

We also saw people who, unbeknownst to any of us, would be purchasing their last gifts.

For example, there was a jovial group of men in the perfume shop buying gifts for their wives. They took their luggage and gifts to their private airplane and buckled in for the short trip to Florida.

As they lifted off, the plane went up and over in a backwards flip. The ties on the rear flaps had not been removed and there was no leveling the plane out. It did a backward loop and crashed to the ground in a ball of fire.

Another major incident hit close to home. A young, French-Canadian, Mr. Chartrand came into the gift shop at the airport, excitedly waving his brand-new pilot's license. He told me he would be flying some people over to Miami to shop for the day and asked if I wanted to join the group.

As a daughter of the Chief of Air Traffic Control, I wisely replied, "No thank you, I would love to go, but your license is too new."

The rest of the group were mainly employees of the Antoni Clinic. Medical technicians, male and female.

After enjoying a fun day of Christmas shopping in Miami, they headed back on their return flight to Freeport. The plane had just made it to the FPO airport, when it crashed. There was no fire.

It had run out of gas.

Dr. Robert Antoni was able to help extricate the one survivor, a young lady who was sitting at the rear of the plane in the jump seat. She had a severe head injury and would spend many weeks in a Miami hospital recovering.

The entire Antoni family came to meet her at the airport when she finally returned to Freeport.

There was a lot of drama in Air Traffic Control for reasons other than plane crashes.

In March of 1970, controllers in the U.S. staged a "sick out" with at least 2,000 controllers calling in sick.

Mom and Daddy had been camping at Roto Rock with some friends. When Daddy went into a small nearby store, he was asked if he was A. R. Smith.

He was told that the Tower in Freeport needed him to return immediately, and a small aircraft was dispatched to fly him to Freeport.

Daddy was very capable, and during another drama in the management of the Tower, he started to resign.

When the other controllers heard that he might step down, they also tendered their resignations in a show of solidarity with him.

The problems were resolved very quickly after that.

Chapter Fifty-nine

Bill Smith and the Haitians

One morning, when my father was working in the Air Traffic Control Tower, an Eastern Airlines pilot reported a "pretty good-sized boat sinking off shore of Freeport." Daddy called for Rescue and all sorts of Emergency vehicles and personnel rushed to the scene.

The Freeport News photographers also headed to the scene as the Yorel II sank.

Rescue quickly helped the men off of the sinking boat. The men were given warm blankets to wrap in, as most were still in underwear. These men were Haitian illegals.

The Captain of the boat, a white man, turned out to be A.R. Smith's new son-in-law, Bill Smith. The next day, a photo of an angry Bill Smith, with his disheveled, dark hair blowing in the wind, appeared on the front page of the Freeport News. Bill Smith was involved in some immature, ridiculous plot to overthrow Haitian leader, "Papa Doc." I think Bill was quoted as saying, "Just shoot me!" If A.R. Smith had been allowed to have a gun in the Bahamas, well…

WILLIAN SMITH hustled ashore by police (above), was master of the Yorel II. Some of the Haitians (below) lost all their clothes- when they abandoned the sinking boat. They were taken to the police station in an ambulance. (Freeport News Photos)

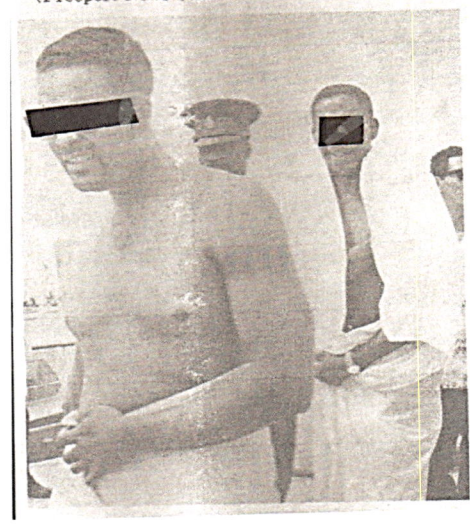

Bill Smith served a short sentence of less than three months in Nassau at Fox Hill prison. The Haitians were deported.

Chapter Sixty

When Bunnies Fly

One day an unusual looking airplane landed at the Freeport International airport. It was a black DC-9, with a white bunny silhouette on the tail.

Hugh Hefner had arrived in Freeport along with several curvy ladies. He and the ladies left the airport to tour Freeport.

Meanwhile, the pilots of the bunny-plane invited my father, A. R. Smith, to come aboard for a tour. They let daddy know that Hefner was scouting locations for another Playboy club.

While my father was aboard the aircraft, a message came in from Hefner that the group was returning to the airport and wanted to leave immediately.

The Captain informed my father that the visit had been cut short because of one of the women using foul language. One of the women had used the such strong profanity everywhere she went, that a police bobby chastised her about it.

She was told to leave.

At that time in Freeport, profanity was rarely ever heard. It was like in the song "Home, Home on the Range." Where seldom is heard, a discouraging word…"

Soon, the black airplane with its 'delightful' bevy of beauties hopped off the island.

Later we learned that a small Playboy club was opened in Freeport. One of its Bunnies was Lauren Hutton who would later become famous as a model.

The Island attracted other famous people, including Howard Hughes, who lived in the Penthouse of the Xanadu.

Mr. and Mrs. Groves lived in the Xanadu Penthouse after Howard Hughes died.

Royalty would visit often. Prince Charles played polo at Pinetree Stable. Prince Rainier and Princess Grace were guests of the Groves.

Above all, Queen Elizabeth II has come to the Islands.

Chapter Sixty-one

Moonlight Ride

One night there was a gigantic full moon, so Pamela and I decided to take a moonlit ride. We went to the stable where we saddled Delilah and Lady Willpower.

Pam said, "I bet the horses are surprised to see us in their stalls this late!" "You're right!" I replied.

We led the horses out of their stalls, and Pam mounted Lady, and I mounted my beloved Delilah.

As we headed the horses down the Pinetree stable driveway, I said, "Hey, the Rectory is right around the corner, let's see if Father Brendan is in. Maybe he will bless the horses!"

Once at the Rectory, we stopped our horses at the front door, where I dismounted and knocked.

Father Brendan opened the door. I could see a troubled-looking woman sitting at a long table just inside the door. I had the impression she was there for counseling.

I probably should have apologized for interrupting his work, but blurted out, "Father Brendan, would it be possible for you to bless our horses?" He was a good sport about it and went back inside just a moment, then came outside with some Holy water. His white hair glistened in the lamplight as he made the sign of the cross and said a few words blessing the horses.

"Thank you, Father Brendan," Pam and I said in unison as we turned the mares toward Sunrise Highway.

The moon lighted the sandy limestone path as the horses walked peacefully along the road. The moonlight also illuminated our golden horses and made their snowy manes shimmer. The night was very quiet with almost no traffic on the highway.

As we rode, I asked Pam, "Your birthday is this weekend, what kind of cake do you want?" She replied, "Yellow cake with milk chocolate icing!"

"Great, I like that too!" I responded.

That weekend, I made a Birthday cake for Pam. Ellen Sheeran, Donna and Christie Hall, and some friends from Spain came to the small gathering.

I drove to the stable and rode Delilah back to the house so that everyone could see her.

Chapter Sixty-two

Pindling

At the height of the incredible success of Freeport, a New Prime Minister, named Lynden Pindling, was elected. His home office was in Nassau. He ran by convincing Bahamians that the jobs would be theirs if he were elected.

The huge success of Freeport had provided thousands of jobs for Bahamians and Freeport also poured approximately 30 to 40 million dollars a year into the rest of the Bahamas. Money that the other Islands could use for schools, hurricane repairs, infrastructure, medical facilities.

At first Pindling was quoted as saying, that he would "not kill 'goose that laid the golden egg'." But, as time passed, he demanded that more jobs go to Bahamians. Upon first glance it seemed like a reasonable request.

However, Pindling did not take into account the time and experience many jobs would require of their applicants.

As a result, many companies were unable to fill positions and these companies left Freeport.

There was also a real brutality to how fast Pindling had work permits taken away from expatriates.

Pindling had his henchmen show up at people's doors, with a letter that stated something to the effect that they had been declared *Undesirable* and would be given two weeks to leave.

One man, named Jim McDougal, owned a large construction company that was in mid-process of building many structures in Freeport. It was devastating to him to have to walk away from the work, not to mention a large number of Bahamians that lost their jobs in construction and countless other jobs.

Some people had to leave so fast, that they had to leave homes and cars behind. Many had no idea what the next day would be like as they loaded what belongings they could take with them and left.

Investors who heard Pindling's "Bend or Break" speech put the brakes on the massive investments in Freeport.

And, in 1973, the Bahamas became Independent from England. While it was great for the pride of the lovely Bahamian people, England had provided a stable, orderliness to the Bahamas.

More importantly, to quote Brit, John Hinchcliffe, "I hope the present Govt. sees the **absolute need** to retain our country's (Britain) presence in the Caribbean and it has to be the Royal Navy…forward defence is vital." (To prevent drug smuggling.)

Investments were backed by England, and the Bahamian police were basically "Bobbies" like the ones in England.

These police didn't carry guns and many rode bicycles in the business areas of Freeport.

Guns were not allowed under British law, but they soon became a common and dangerous part of Freeport.

Worst of all "there was a tangible 'anti-white' feeling on the Island…although many locals were easy going, responsive and likeable. This negative attitude was actively encouraged by the political power at the time under the Premiership of Lynden, later Sir Lynden Pindling…it was a political tool."

A wild west attitude took hold.

For example, the incredibly important Deep-water Port was very well-run by Port Director, John Hinchcliffe, whom Hayward had hired out of England. Hinchcliffe arrived to a Port that was "run down, business weak, and low morale."

Soon after Hinchcliffe started, in 1980, about 144,000 passengers arrived at the harbor. By 1988, the number of passengers numbered at 740,000!

However, when taxis were required to line up in an orderly sequence, to pick up tourists some drivers would cut in line, and some would refuse to help carry luggage for the thousands of tourists that poured into Freeport.

A massive drug trade developed in Freeport, a lot of it being dealt at the dock, and ships full of hidden drugs heading to Florida, regularly played cat-and-mouse with the U.S. Coast Guard.

Pindling had already taken control of the police department from the Port Authority, and when John Hinchcliffe tried to get the Police involved to bring order to the Dock area, the problems were never addressed.

As a result of the chaos and threats to his and his family's safety, the incredibly competent and valiant John Hinchcliffe resigned.

The Prime Minister that followed Pindling, Sir Hubert Ingraham noted the damage to the Islands thus, "This far-reaching and destructive ways, those roots sank deep into our culture feeding off and growing from the rampant **drug trafficking and gangsterism which ran wild in the 70s and 80s.**"

In the book, "A Nation for Sale," the corruption in the Bahamas was written about extensively, using a lot of investigative excerpts from the Miami Herald.

"High-level corruption in the Bahamas directly affects the flow of drugs to American shores; more importantly, it endangers the future of 223,000 Bahamians."

"For most of them, who have worked hard and rejoiced in their country's independence, drug corruption has brought shame, misery and an unprecedented crisis of leadership."

Miami Herald article 1976

Chapter Sixty-three

Storm Clouds at Stable

The young girl ran sobbing from the stable manager's office, her blond hair flying as she ran to her Mom's car. Her Mother, followed behind her.

They were upset that they would lose their horse.

The family was having to leave the Island and leave so quickly that they had to give their horse back to the stable. They could not take their lovely gelding with them.

It would likely live out its years being rented to be ridden by tourists.

I saw this small drama play out, yet I was oblivious that the incident had anything to do with my life.

Or Delilah's fate.

JOHN SCOTT, senior systems analyst at IDP, explains advanced computer techniques to twins Brenda and Linda Smith, junior programmers. Brenda is standing. The twins are 1968 graduages of Freeport High School.

Chapter Sixty-four

Lose Job

There were storm clouds at our job, also. Like hundreds of other companies, we discovered that Island Data Processing would be leaving Freeport.

One day when we went to work, we were informed that the company was having to close in Freeport. They said we would be given the best of references, but that didn't make us feel better.

Both Brenda and I realized that I *COULD* lose Delilah! The thought was as inconceivable as if I had a young child that I was told to walk away from.

Delilah was as much a part of me as the air I breathed.

We were one.

Both Brenda and I were frantic at the thought. To make matters worse, our father wanted us to leave almost immediately.

We were rushing to find out how to ship Delilah, and where to ship her, and keep her safe.

Chapter Sixty-five

Trying to Ship Delilah

The most logical place to ship Delilah would be to Miami. I talked to Customs in Miami to find out how to ship Delilah.

Brenda and I made many phone calls from pay phones trying to figure out what to do. We were afraid to put any long-distance calls on the house phone.

One problem after another occurred.

Miami Customs told me that no horses were being allowed into Miami, as six horses from the Dominican Republic had come in to the facility with an infectious disease.

Quarantine couldn't accept more horses for an indefinite period of time.

The next entry to the U.S. would have to be out of some large city such as New York, which would be impossible for me to go up there and ship Delilah to Miami.

As I made phone calls, Brenda stood outside of the booth with her fingers crossed. She told me that every penny she had was mine to help get Delilah off the Island.

Even with Brenda's help, I was quickly running out of money to continue boarding Delilah as I was longer working.

Although we had always been wonderful daughters and gave our parents no trouble, in fact most people would have loved to have us as their daughters, we knew Daddy would not help us.

You could not get between him and money.

I was terrified that I would have to do what the young girl who ran from the stable office; just walk away.

Horrible thoughts haunted me.

I was afraid Delilah would have to become a rental horse again and could possibly be killed in traffic the way Sandy Man was!

I was beside myself with worry - I *had* to protect Delilah!

Chapter Sixty-six

Testimonial Dinner

Brenda and I decided to go to the Testimonial Dinner that was to honor Garnet J. Levarity. Mr. Levarity, a Bahamian and former Head of the Police, had been bestowed the Order of the British Empire by Her Majesty, Queen Elizabeth II, due to his superior service, and humanity, as well as his common sense.

Levarity was a man who could be depended on if you had any problems in Freeport that required law enforcement. For example, our elder sister, Carole, had a certain man become obsessed with her. He had even been known to break into our house.

Our father, who is an unusually tough man, got into a fight with this much younger, much stronger man. The fight ended with Daddy telling the man, "I will let you live, *this time.*"

One call to Levarity, and the next day, the stalker was seen being dragged through the airport by two Bahamian Police Officers.

He was deported that day.

Brenda decided to wear her new black jumpsuit to the affair. She slipped into the black jumpsuit and zipped it up the front, then she put on her black heels.

Brenda truly looked like a "Bond" girl. Her figure was absolute perfection, and she had one of the most beautiful faces imaginable. Her eyes are hazel-green, and sometimes emerald depending on the light. Brenda looked a lot like Brigette Bardot if Bardot had sun-highlighted brown hair and green eyes. Yet, Brenda was as guileless/smart as she could be.

We were both young *ladies* who had very little dating experience other than the occasional Prom date.

I dressed in a white knit dress and white patent heels. When I touched up my makeup, one of my false eyelashes kept refusing to stay in place. I finally wrangled it into place, and we left for the evening's festivities.

The Camelot room had two large ballrooms ready to accommodate the approximately 600 guests. Each room had large, round tables with red tablecloths and silver candles. Every place setting included three wine glasses and a champagne glass.

Brenda and I, as well as six other guests, shared a large,

round table. The centerpiece on the table was made up of beautiful tropical flowers in yellow, red, and purple colors.

We settled in to enjoy an incredible dinner.

Soup was served with Wyld's Bristol Sherry.

While speakers regaled the audience with anecdotes about Levarity, Salmon Mousseline Chantilly was served with Champagne. After that, the main course of Roasted Larded Tenderloin was served with Springen Reh 1966.

The rather good-looking man to Brenda's right wore a gold watch that gleamed softly as he cut into the beef. Brenda complimented it, "What a beautiful watch. I love its coin face."

The man gingerly removed it from his wrist, stared at Brenda, and placed it on the table in front of Brenda's plate.

An offering.

Brenda calmly took a sip of Champagne from a crystal goblet.

I sipped Beaujolais De Beaune.

I'm sure the other guests at our table wondered if Brenda would accept the gold watch. The man told her, "It's yours. What's five-grand to me?"

The watch set in front of Brenda's plate for the rest of the evening, glowing as only gold does.

It was there when we ate dessert of Bombe Glacee Levarity, and Petit Fours.

It was still there, when we left the table to join other guests at the soiree' for after dinner refreshments.

Meanwhile, Dr. Robert left the dinner.

All female eyes followed his tuxedoed figure as he crossed the Camelot Room of the King's Inn Hotel and left through the double Ballroom doors.

He was leaving the dinner early, very likely to handle a medical emergency.

Our ex-boss from Island Data Processing walked by and saw Brenda and me. He hesitated for a moment and put a hand on Brenda's hip, and whispered, "If you had dressed like this at work…"

She carefully brushed his hand from her hip and we continued mingling with the otherwise well-behaved crowd.

We were introduced to a gorgeous young couple, Sue and Bob Rimmer. Sue looked a lot like the actress, Katherine Ross.

She was slender and had the thickest mane of long chestnut hair.

Bob was a handsome man with thick blond hair, and a winning smile.

We talked about the evening, and I told them about my beautiful Delilah.

Sue said, "Oh, I have always loved horses!"

I said, "Well, Bob and Sue, come to Pinetree Stables and I will show you Delilah."

Chapter Sixty-seven

Push Comes to Shove

Unfortunately, Brenda and I found ourselves in a terrible situation. We were trying everything to put together a plan to ship Delilah, when I overheard my father say "he wanted us to leave as soon as possible."

He couldn't stand the thought of me spending *my* money to keep Delilah.

I had never stood up to him in my life, but when it came to my beloved horse, I got into a terrible fight with him. Still, he planned to put us on planes to the states *Asap*.

I was about to be forced to walk away from Delilah and just give her back to the stable.

Brenda was sent away first. She went to our Grandmother in lonely Memphis.

She only had enough money to take a cab from the airport.

At the last minute, just a day before I had to get on a plane, I called Sue and Bob Rimmer. I knew they had fallen in love with Delilah.

I could never sell Delilah, but I did ask them to pay her final feed bill from Pinetree Stable.

It was around $300.

I told them, "You don't know what you are getting, and when you know, you won't be able to part with her, so I want the right to breed her at some point and get a foal for me."

At this point, Delilah seemed to know something was up.

No one from the stable could load her into a trailer to move her to Eight-Mile Rock. I had to get into the horse trailer, and she quickly came into it with me.

I had to betray her.

Once at Eight-Mile Rock, I put Delilah into the shipping crate that would be her new stall.

Everyone was watching me.

I could not say goodbye, all I could do was turn away and walk in stiff steps as I fought back all of the emotions in me.

Chapter Sixty-eight

Delilah in Misery

Delilah was miserable at Eight-Mile Rock. She was completely alone in a small pen that had a shipping crate in the corner which was her makeshift stall. She had reverted to the way she looked when I first bought her-skinny and depressed. The light was gone from her eyes.

She looked like a dead horse propped up by four legs.

She didn't just look terrible, she was behaving in a way I had never imagined she could.

Sue told me that Delilah *bit* and *kicked* her. I was incredulous. As she told me, I kept repeating, "Delilah? Delilah! Delilah was a gentle angel that I could trust around children. They could safely go into her stall and brush her.

Sue was a good person and for Delilah to purposely kick or bite at Sue meant Delilah was as miserable and as devastated as I.

How could Delilah know I had no choice? I knew with so many horses being returned to the stable, that she could end up being ridden by tourists, and perhaps be killed in traffic.

I was in deep distress over leaving Delilah. And she was in distress being separated from me.

In her distress, Delilah even stepped on Sue's foot, injuring it.

I always tell people that if a horse steps on its owner's foot, it is on purpose. Horses know where their feet are!

After a very rocky start in the U.S., I made my way to Miami and worked at a bank. For the next two years, I flew into Freeport monthly and rode Delilah.

When it was time for me to leave, Delilah would put her neck over my shoulder and almost seemed to be trying to hold me close to her.

One day when I wasn't on the Island, Delilah got so upset that she jumped the chain-link fence of her pen and ran across a golf course, churning up the greens as she went.

She ran onto the beach and was finally caught by a tourist who kept exclaiming, "She is so beautiful, she is so beautiful!"

I was told she was headed in the direction of Freeport and may have been trying to get back to Pinetree Stables.

Thankfully Sue moved her back to Pinetree Stables.

Delilah looking longingly at grass…

Chapter Sixty-nine

When Horses Fly

By now, both Sue and Bob had left Freeport, but made plans to ship Delilah out. I insisted that I fly with Delilah to ensure her safety.

I met the plane in Miami in the predawn hours. I could see that the battery was being jumped by a ground battery. Not a good sign. The pilot and co-pilot were a couple of English chaps. They expected me and we set off for Freeport as the sun was rising. I took a cab to the stable, where two horses were already in the two-horse trailer.

There was no room for Delilah, so they would have to make a second trip to pick her up. "Don't worry, I will just ride her to the airport." I said.

I rode Delilah bareback the several miles to the airport. She was always so content and trusting, where I was concerned, and faithfully carried me for our last ride. I looked at her white mane blowing slightly in the breeze and her golden neck and ears. "I

Love you, Delilah, please forgive me. No one is keeping me safe, but I can keep YOU safe! Sue and Bob will be good to you." I said, as I tried to memorize every gold and white hair on her.

After going about five miles, we were at the airport where I dismounted and led her out onto the tarmac. The first two horses were in a crate which was fork lifted into the cargo hold of the plane. Then it was Delilah's turn. She was almost too big to fit through the cargo door. A couple of men gently lowered her head and were careful she was not injured as the crate was moved into the hold.

Once inside, she was situated between the other two horses, probably to balance the weight properly. She had a hay bag hanging near her.

Each horse had a chain through its halter, so they could not lift their heads higher than level. They also had straps across their backs to keep them secured in the snug crates.

I boarded the cargo plane. Delilah wouldn't take her eyes off of me as I stared at her wondering how I would live without her.

It was getting very hot in the aircraft.

The pilot said, "Have some hot tea, it will cool you off."

I was puzzled by him telling me that a hot drink would cool me off, but I replied, "Thanks, I will try it!"

He handed me a cup of hot tea, after adding some milk to it. I actually started to feel cooler!

When we landed in Miami, an elderly Veterinarian perused the paperwork on the horses. He turned to me and said the papers were incomplete and the horses would have to return to Freeport!

I am usually not very assertive, but I quickly found the words, "NO, they can't go back, it is too HOT and they will die!"

The Vet was reasonable. After a few phone calls, we got the paperwork sent from Freeport.

Vet Assistants had already unloaded the horses.

Delilah was led into the large, warehouse-type room where I was waiting. The Vet took her temperature the usual way. There was a string on the thermometer with a clip on the end. The Vet attached the clip to Delilah's white tail while the thermometer registered her temperature. He then put a liquid in her ears, I think to kill any mites.

Afterwards, Delilah was led to a metal holding device and was thoroughly washed with spray hoses.

Her hooves were also disinfected. Each hoof was cleaned and a disinfectant was slathered onto it. After this, she was led to a second room and her hooves were cleaned again. Finally, she was put into a clean stall with fresh hay and water. The stall had a metal door, with a small window that had bars on it and I could see into her stall.

I noticed there were tropical birds in the stall next to her.

One of the men told me that all sorts of animals come through quarantine. He told me that the famous race horse, Canonero, had come through this same facility.

I watched Delilah through the small window to her stall, as she settled in. She would be in quarantine for a week.

I stared at her beautiful, golden body and exquisite face as she ate hay.

I didn't cry as I left the airport and took a taxi back to where I was staying in Miami.

Somehow my grief had frozen in place.

The only respite I had was in my loving dreams of Delilah.

I wrote a poem inspired by Delilah Merrygold, and our days at Silver Cove.

Silver Cove

She died in the sand

A horseshoe in her hand

Lying stretched on her side

Peaceful as the lapping tide

Silver Cove welcomed her home

Her golden mare shone

It so graceful arrived

With the promise realized

White hooves shod with three –

And one from me…

Chapter Seventy

Wallace Groves' Funeral

The following is from Brenda's diary.

Brenda Smith Copeland

11:12 a.m. EST

9:15 p.m. First leg of trip to Freeport on a Delta airline Memphis to Atlanta. I'm writing this aboard the plane. There are 169 passengers on this flight – 75,000 gallons of fuel, 37,000 feet altitude. The plane is large, with seven seats across and movie screens on the back of every seat. I'm hungry. I worked all day, and had neither breakfast nor dinner, went to a Fedex Management class, and caught this flight. They only served us peanuts!

In Atlanta, my sister, Carole and her daughter Angela, picked me up at the airport. Angela is the best little girl ever! She is beautiful, sweet, smart, and affectionate. Carole is wonderful, too. I spent the night at Carole's home. Her home is so 'homey' with lace everywhere, pillows, pictures. Carole is fabulous – in a way that can't be bought at a store.

Next day:

I'm now on the second leg of my trip. I'm writing this aboard a Delta L1011 flying from Atlanta to Miami. In Miami, I will catch an Eastern airline to Freeport Grand Bahama for Mr. Groves' funeral. I keep humming "Sentimental Journey."

Despite the reason for my trip, it's always a dream to return to Freeport, because I feel as if I am coming home. So far so good, until my flight from Miami to Freeport is delayed from a 2:06 p.m. arrival to a 2:45 arrival. The funeral is at 3:00! I am a nervous wreck and am getting a stress headache. The Eastern Airlines plane (that had chipped blue paint on its nose) was replaced by another EAL aircraft, and I finally boarded the aircraft for the 23-minute flight to Freeport.

For a magical moment, a circular rainbow surrounded the shadow of the airplane on the water. I took it as a sign of the "Magic City of Freeport" and its Founder, Wallace Groves.

About half-way to Freeport, I felt the invisible barrier between the hectic world of the U.S. fade away and the beloved, enchanting world of Freeport come into view.

In Bahamian Customs, I said that I was there for Mr. Groves' funeral. The Customs agent cleared me immediately without checking my baggage (and that's how I smuggled the 50 pounds of cocaine onto the Island Your Honor – just kidding!) Outside of Customs, I told the friendly Bahamian that I needed a taxi to Groves' funeral. He quickly hailed a cab as he said, "No Problem!" (the famous Bahamian attitude) as respect for Mr. Groves.

The taxi driver drove to Mary Star of the Sea Catholic Church on East Sunrise Highway. I noticed how much bigger the trees have gotten since I was in Freeport. The landscaping was beautiful along the highway, and I noticed a few new buildings. The taxi arrived at the Church *just* as the Priests were about to head for the entrance.

I dashed ahead of them with my carry-on luggage in hand. I had no time to put it anywhere. I ran into guess who? Dr. Robert – who looked just like Omar Sharif. (Our family loves him so, and he is a beloved member of the Freeport community.)

Dr. Robert said he was glad to see me and kissed me on the cheek! I found a seat and sat down. The Church is round and has red carpet. It is beautiful and was packed with people. After a few minutes the Groves' children, Gene, Gayle, Gordon, Gary, and

Graham walked in. Their mother, Georgette Groves, had died about a year ago.

Dr. Robert kissed Gene on the cheek. She looked so thin, elegant, and a little pained. She didn't see me as she walked past.

Dr. Amado sat directly behind me. Dr. Amado is the handsome brother of Dr. Robert and is father to Melanie and Kirk Antoni.

The service began with the Priest saying that Father Brendan regretted that he could not be there. Father Brendan was the original Priest that we had for all the years in Freeport. His health was failing and I am sure he would have loved to officiate Mr. Groves' funeral.

Members of the Bahamian Parliament and Prime Minister Lynden Pindling were present.

The pallbearers included Gordon and Gary Groves. I was very touched to see the elderly, white-haired friend of Mr. Groves, Keith Gonsalves, acting as a pallbearer. Mr. Gonsalves was bent in half by back problems, but he still made the effort to honor his friend.

The Priest and others talked about Mr. Groves. The Priest said that Mr. Groves was the creator of the "Magic City of Freeport." How true! There were also representatives from Georgetown University in Washington D.C. One talked about how Wallace Groves had earned five degrees in two years at the University – three degrees one year, and two the next! Groves was referred to as the "Boy genius."

Sister Mary Alice, the head Nun from Mary Star of the Sea, spoke of Wallace Groves, saying he loved children and talked about them as being the future. Sister Mary Alice is very old, white-haired, and almost blind – she wore large black glasses and a black and white habit. Her voice cracked at the end.

Another person, a man, spoke about Wallace Groves starting the 'Freeport Dream' at the age of 54. Everyone thought it would fail as so many "Out Island" projects had. Mr. Groves brought very talented investors such as D.K. Ludwig and Keith Gonsalves in.

This man also shared a story about going fishing with Mr. Groves. Mr. Groves cracked open a conch, and said, "would you like to eat some bait?"

Several people talked about how generous Mr. Groves was in private. He helped many people in Freeport, but quietly with no fanfare.

Mr. Groves loved his wife Georgette. Linda and I have seen their obvious bond during the years we visited or traveled with them.

One Priest talked about the severe grief Mr. Groves suffered when Georgette died last year.

Dr. Amado was standing in line for Communion. He looked striking with his black hair and white tropical suit.

After the service, the Priest had everyone shake hands with each other.

A 90- year-old Bahamian woman stood next to me. She and several other people were crying. I asked her how long she had known Mr. Groves. She told me she knew and loved Wallace Groves from the time he owned the Abaco Lumber Company in the 1950's. She said Mr. and Mrs. Groves loved children, and always had a big Christmas party every year for the employees and their children.

After red roses were placed on the bronze casket, we all proceeded to leave the Church. Dr. Robert was shaking hands with each person as they left. He kissed me and said I was beautiful. I told him he was too. A man standing next to him asked who the pretty woman was (me?) and Dr. Robert said, "We're good friends."

I said, "Definitely!"

As I walked outside of the Church, into the sunlight, I saw hundreds of people milling around. I scanned the crowd for Gene. I saw her across the driveway in a black limousine. I started waving, just slowly, hoping she would see me in the crowd. All of a sudden, she started jumping up and down in the car. I wasn't sure if she saw me until she jumped out of the limo. It was just like one of those slow-motion movie scenes of her running to me, and me trying to run through the crowd to her. She rushed up to me, and said, "You made it!" We hugged so tightly – just couldn't let go. We were both crying.

When we stopped hugging, she said she thought all of her crying was over – that she thought she had done all her crying. She asked if I had tissues, which I did and got one for each of us. I said I would trade them for an aspirin since I had such a bad headache. I showed her my suitcase and said I had just come from the airport.

She said, "How are we going to get you to the Lucayan Country Club?"

Melanie Antoni Malone and her husband, Don, were standing nearby. They saw us hugging and walked over to speak to Gene. Melanie insisted on giving me a ride to the Lucayan Country Club. Gene said, "Good, it's that or the trunk of the limo!" Same old nut!

I walked with Melanie and Don to their Z28. Melanie got into the back seat. She is so stylish of course and looks a little like Marie Osmond, only much prettier. She also has an exquisite speaking voice!

She told me that her brother, Kirk, is in England studying Law. He will take the bar exam in six months and is married to an English girl.

Melanie has been married for thirteen years and has an eight-year-old daughter. Melanie and Don dropped me at the entrance to the Lucayan Country Club.

Gene was already there and greeted me with an outstretched palm with three aspirins in it!

Gene and I went inside where bartenders served us champagne from behind a circular bar. The Lucayan Country Club has enormous windows on three sides, giving a panoramic view of the beautiful Lucayan Country Club's emerald-green golf course.

Gary Groves approached me. He said, "I remember you!" I said, "I remember you too, and you look as mischievous as ever."

Gary is red-haired with freckles and has a great Leprechaun twinkle in his eyes.

I sat with Gayle Groves and the rest of the family. Gayle is married to a handsome Brit named David.

There was a buffet set up with turkeys, hams, roast beef, and other delicacies. Hibiscus flowers and greenery were woven throughout the buffet and on the tables. I love hibiscus, and they are so fitting for an Island funeral.

Afterwards, I still had to catch my return flight to the U.S. Gene asked someone for their rental car keys and we left in the small car. I told Gene that I couldn't leave Freeport without going into the water.

She drove to the nearby Lucayan Beach Hotel and we walked to the water's edge. I took my shoes off, and although I still had stockings on, I walked into the water and marveled at the aqua paradise in front of me. The familiar, warm aqua water and white sand was glorious!

We returned to the car and Gene drove me, in my wet, sandy stockings to the airport. The sun was setting.

Of course…

Epilogue

Like so many of the people that loved Freeport, Brenda and I never really felt at home in any other place after we left.

Fortunately, we were able to keep in touch with many of our old friends in Freeport, including Gene Groves. We still visit her, and we have spent a lot of time over the years in the Bahamas and several other places with her.

Gene's perseverance in learning to cook, paid off. She is known for making a fantastic Christmas pudding every year. I should say, many Christmas puddings.

Her siblings, as well as her nieces and nephews are always urging her to make even more of the flaming dessert. The puddings have really become a delicious family tradition thanks to Gene.

Gene spends a lot of her time helping in every way possible at a dog rescue in the Northeast. She is very passionate about the Rescue and extremely devoted to aiding the dogs.

Gene has also been the most incredible friend to me and Brenda. She has always rolled out the Red Carpet for us and makes us feel like the most "Important" people in the room when we are around her. She has been the most loyal and treasured friend to us.

Mr. Ray McNeill eventually became the Headmaster of Freeport High School, and also became a beloved friend of ours for life.

Brenda and I remained friends with him and his wonderful wife, artist Doreen McNeill, until Ray died a few years ago in New Zealand. He was always our staunchest supporter, saying he had "never seen the kind of potential Brenda and I had."

Mr. Groves was unscathed by the changes in Freeport. He managed to sell his part of the Grand Bahama Development Company for 80 million dollars early, before much damage was done to Freeport.

He and his beloved Georgette Groves lived in Miami and travelled between Miami and Freeport for years.

The Groves were large financial supporters of the Rosenstiel School of Marine and Atmospheric Science on Virginia Key, and the Miami Heart Institute which named a wing after Mr. Groves.

The University of Georgetown in Washington also named a Hall for Mr. Groves.

One of the most important things the Groves did was to start a scholarship program for Bahamian students. It has helped many students pay for college over the last several decades.

Myra Wagener went on to work in several of the finest equestrian areas in the U.S. We are all so proud to learn that she won the Dressage Century Award in 2016.

The award is rare, as it requires the age of the rider, and the age of the horse to add up to one hundred! Myra found a 26-year-old dressage horse nicknamed, "Charlie" when she was 74, and won the competition!

My hat is off to her!

Everyone's hat is also off to the legendary Antoni Doctors - Doctors Robert, Amado, and Albert.

Dr. Robert Antoni was recently bestowed the OBE, The Order of The British Empire at Buckingham Palace for his humanitarian work in the Bahamas.

Well done, Doctor Robert!

My budding relationship with Miles Berkeley was definitely impacted by the loss of Freeport.

I moved many times when I first moved to the U.S. having no idea what to do after my traumatic loss of home and horse. Miles would try to visit me, and did come to see me in San Jose, California where I was jettisoned.

He continued to write me for twelve years, and I had started dating a very talented singer named Gary Young.

Miles was dating someone else, also, and made a final call to me to see if I was still with Gary. I said yes, and he went ahead and married the woman he was with at the time.

Theirs was a short marriage, that produced a very talented son, who is a fantastic photographer in London.

I married and eventually divorced Gary.

He is a special and talented person in his own right, and we treasure the friendship we have now. He is one of my most treasured friends.

Miles and I found each other again in 2009 and were beside ourselves with excitement.

Then, one day he asked me to call him in England. He said he was taking a trip, and "wanted to take my voice with him." I didn't call right away, then I didn't hear from him.

The day he had asked me to call him, he had already checked into a hotel, left a letter to his barrister, and took a gas that is available to scuba divers, knowing it would end his life.

I was devastated.

His best friend contacted me and explained that it had nothing to do with me not calling.

Miles had developed a very serious heart condition. In fact, he had suffered five heart attacks in one day! Miles knew he was dying, and with the strict, orderly stiff-upper-lip of the Brits, he bowed out.

I am beyond honored that he wanted to "take my voice with him."

As for Freeport, the beloved place with wonderful people continued a free-fall worse than anyone could have imagined.

Instead of an incredibly vibrant, safe tourist destination, full of investors, and streets "paved in gold' Pindling ushered in an era of rampant drug trade, crime, and corruption.

The immaculate landscaping from the airport to the Lucayan Beach is no more. Most of the original landmarks are overgrown and unrecognizable, if they are standing at all.

Almost all of the great hotels and casinos have fallen into ruin.

Even mansions are abandoned or bull dozed, including the Groves' mansion on the beach, many years after they sold it.

The stunning International Bazaar is a skeletal remain of buildings that have become sites for drug use and homeless people.

The giant green Hoi Toi (the Budda) managed to stand until recently when someone toppled it to the ground.

The few men that still own taxis, often live in those taxis.

When I visit, I see a sadness in many of the wonderful Bahamians. When I mention I am from the old days in Freeport, they wistfully say, "Come back…"

There is, however, hope for Freeport. After all, it is still incredibly well located near the U.S. to become a successful tourist hot spot. It still has the beautiful ocean and friendly people. And it is still deeply loved by the expatriates and Bahamians alike.

Pindling died wealthy while many Bahamians became homeless.

Many of our peers, our friends and fellow students, have also felt the terrible loss of our "home." No matter what flag it flew, Freeport was *home*.

We have all missed it beyond the understanding of people who are not Freeporters.

Sad to think that not only did we need Freeport all our lives, but Freeport clearly needed us to continue to be part of it. It suffered even more than we did.

As for our Dad, he changed almost completely as he grew older. It was as if he woke up to the error of making money the most important thing in life.

A light seemed to come on in him, and he became approachable and enjoyable to be around.

He said that tightly holding on to money was foolish. He *TRULY* understood, and could be heard lecturing younger men that were going down his same path. He said all it did was lead to trying to keep attorneys or nursing homes from getting it.

We were not close when we were young, but after he "woke up" we grew to love and understand him.

He also seemed to really appreciate us and could often be heard bragging about us.

And we certainly appreciated all he had done for the family, as far as the fascinating places we lived, and the beautiful homes in which we lived.

As far as my beloved Delilah, I continued to dream about her for decades. Dreams of riding her, or just being with her. My last dream of her was of horse bones in the grass...

Although I owned a couple of horses during that time, I was still looking for a "gaited palomino mare."

As usual, my great twin, Brenda, came to the rescue. She called one day and wanted us to drive to Alabama where an older man named Jim Ash was reducing the size of his herd.

Brenda said, "He has a palomino mare."

When I first saw Design, I started shaking, afraid Mr. Ash would change his mind about selling her. Design had a white blaze that was identical to the top half of Delilah's blaze, and she had identical white stockings on her hind legs as Delilah.

She was for sale, though, and what was even more exciting is she was in foal to a World Champion Tennessee Walker named Electrifying.

Mr. Ash said he would deliver her to me in Florida in about two weeks.

Honestly, I wasn't sure I could stay alive for two more weeks waiting to reach out and take the lead rope from Mr. Ash!

Jim Ash delivered Design as promised, and once he led her out of the horse trailer, he handed me the lead rope.

In…excruciatingly… slow… motion.

It seemed like an eternity rather than just seconds for me to wrap my fingers around the rope with my new golden mare on the end of it.

Design was so similar to Delilah that I would tell people I wasn't sure she wasn't Delilah. Especially the day I was working in a cramped area near a horse trailer.

It was hard for me to fit into the area.

Suddenly, Design, whom I had only had for a few weeks, hurried over to me and wedged herself in the tight area with me and buried her muzzle in my neck.

Like a kiss.

Like a reunion with an old friend.

It was as if she suddenly recognized me.

In the dreams I had after buying Design, the horse in it was now Design!

One night, I even dreamed of her foal before she had him.

Brenda had hoped Design would foal a palomino filly, which she would buy from me. However, I had a dream, where I saw a sorrel colt lying next to Design.

The next day, I told Brenda, "You won't get your palomino filly, I saw a sorrel colt, and he will be born on Daddy's Birthday, March 9."

That's exactly what happened.

Unbelievably, he has a white mark on his nose in the shape of Grand Bahama!

And what did we name the big sorrel colt? His name is...

"Freeport Forever!"

Thanks to everyone who showed such interest in Dreamhorse Bahamas.

A very special thanks to Gene Groves, Myra Wagener, Melanie Margo Antoni, John Hinchcliffe, and Donna Hall.

Thanks, too, to Daddy (A.R. Smith) for his stories of the dramas in Air Traffic Control in Freeport.

We Love You!

I also want to thank my beloved twin, Brenda Copeland, who added so many of her own Memoirs, that we were able to co-author Dreamhorse Bahamas.

All my love to my unforgettable Delilah…

Brenda on left, Linda on right

doveisfive@outlook.com or Brendacopeland1950@outlook.com

Made in the USA
Lexington, KY
29 November 2018